MW00849312

Life is My Guru

A Practical Guide

To Understanding What Your Life Experiences
Are Trying To Teach You

Dr. Bobby J. Price

Life is My Guru: A Practical Guide To Understanding What Your Life Experiences Are Trying To Teach You

Copyright ©2022 Wise Old Owl Publishing

All rights reserved. No part of this publication may be reproduced or transmitted in any form or by any means, physical or electronic, including photocopying and recording, or by any information storage and retrieval systems, without written permission from the author or publisher. Except in the case of brief quotations or short video clips embodied in critical articles or reviews.

Paperback ISBN: 978-0-9996124-2-2

Hardcover ISBN: 978-0-9996124-3-9

Creative Writing Consultant: C. Nzingha Smith

Editor: Carla DuPont

DISCLAIMER

The advice and strategies contained herein may not be suitable for every situation. This work is sold with the understanding that the Author and Publisher are not engaged in rendering legal, accounting, or professional services.

Neither the Author nor the Publisher shall be liable for any damages arising here from. The fact that an organization or website is referred to in this work as a citation or a potential source of further information is not a direct endorsement of the information that the organization or website may provide or recommendations it may make to individuals by the Author or Publisher.

Further, readers should be aware that the internet websites listed in this work may have changed or disappeared between when this work was written, published, and read.

DEDICATION

This book is dedicated to one of my greatest teachers, my father, Bobby Price. My life is a continuum of your wildest dreams only because of your unwavering devotion to me. Your presence and love was always an anchor, sail, and a guiding light that showed me the way to becoming a good man. Thank you for being the often uncelebrated soil and foundation that builds character and strength in children. You gave me two of the greatest gifts a son can ever receive: believing in myself and knowing you were proud of me.

They say when a good father transitions, a part of his child dies and a part of the father lives on in his child forever. I pray that you will remain with me every remaining step of my journey until we reunite again in the spiritual plane.

CONTENTS

INTRODUCTION

Writing this book was both painful and cathartic. Initially, I was writing an entirely different book on healing to follow up on my first book, *Vegucation Over Medication*. But every time I sat down to write, the only thoughts I could download were the contents for this book. All my life experiences kept flashing across my mind like a carefully composed string of events to ultimately give me the moral of my life's story.

We all have a beautiful story to tell full of tragedy, triumph, and mystery. This book isn't just about the stories of my life, it's about the awakening that occurs when we turn inward. When we allow our awareness to shed light on the darkest parts of ourselves that we've disowned, disliked, and swept under the rug. This is the "shadow work" we must complete while here on earth. Our traumas and dramas leave lasting marks on our souls that have hidden consequences on who we believe we are and how we respond to our life experiences.

James Baldwin said, "To be a negro in this country and to be relatively conscious is to be in a state of rage, almost all the time."

I've always had a certain consciousness about my life experiences, even as a child, that I felt no one else had. There was a time I knew exactly who I was. During that same time, I never remember looking in the mirror thinking about what someone else thought about me or questioning what I should or shouldn't be doing.

Most of who and what we think we are, are just layers of masks stacked on top of each other. Each mask represents a personality trait we created to cover up the pain of a previous traumatic experience. The masks help us survive the experience in the moment but will eventually lead to DIS-EASE (creating disharmony or anxiety) in the body later in life.

The stress of physical or emotional trauma has an equally damaging effect on the body's wellness. Short-term stress will make us more fit for survival. But when the stress is constant or too traumatic, it impacts our physiology and psychology long-term. So, stress can create DIS-EASE (lack of peace) in the body. A great example would be HYPER-TENSION (too much tension), also known as high blood pressure or the silent assassin.

Early childhood trauma can also create unconscious behaviors like disconnection. These days, it's common to see a small child disconnected and consider it as normal. Later in life, the disconnection, lack of affection, and inability to focus is called Attention Deficit Disorder (ADD).

Much of the shadow work we need to do as adults originated from childhood traumas. Our survival response to that trauma creates conditioning and programming that continually plays out in our adult lives. We see these conditioned responses in our life experiences when triggered emotions are reminiscent of the original trauma. We also see these impulsive, automated reactions whenever a situation uncovers parts of ourselves that we refuse to confront. The programming tells us what to think, how to feel, and the choices we should make without us even thinking.

I learned that this was my truth while writing this book. The more I wrote, the more I realized I didn't need to heal the man I'd become. It was the 12-year-old version of myself that was wreaking most of the havoc in my life that needed the healing.

To start my healing process, I realized I had to remove the comfort of victimhood and view my life, both past and present, objectively. It was time to have conversations I had refused to have with people I didn't want to talk to. This was one light of enlightenment that helped me understand how worthy of a journey this would be.

One of my biggest epiphanies was when I discovered that, in some cases, I had completely erased some of my memories because they were so traumatic. In other cases, I created an entirely new false version of reality to cope. That was the first time I realized my memory and my thoughts were unreliable for understanding my own life. The only thing I could truly trust was my awareness. In so many ways, this book was the understanding and therapy I always wished I was brave enough to find.

Over a decade ago, my physical decline in health inspired me to adopt a healthier, more holistic way of living. It changed my life in every way I could never imagine. It not only created more peace in my body, but that harmony extended to my emotional and mental well-being also. This gave me the strength and courage to embark upon my greatest challenge in life: to heal my broken spirit. Writing this book has expanded my understanding of what it means to heal holistically and become whole again.

I now realize that without the content and lessons I share in this book, I would've never been able to write my first book. Because it was these life lessons that allowed me to love myself enough to eat and live healthier.

Changing my lifestyle shifted my perception of how life was happening. It gave me a completely new set of lenses to view my life experiences. With my old set of bifocals, I could only see life from the perspective of cause-and-effect, or shit happens. With my new multi-sensory lenses, I am able to see an all-encompassing bigger picture related to my collective experiences.

I spent most of my life thinking bad luck and misfortune were always lurking around the corner. On any rare occasion that I experienced joy, I would instantly brace myself for the inevitable bullshit. This prevented me from fully enjoying relationships, compliments, accomplishments, and even laughter. This is the self-inflicted uncaged prison that many of us are living in right now as I write. Unable to live authentically, fully, or freely because conditioning created by thoughts and emotions derived from past traumas keeps us bound.

Life Is My Guru is a roadmap on how to return to your authentic self. I'll illustrate by using my own personal traumas and tragedies. Then, I'll explain how I shifted my thinking to pull the wisdom out of each experience and discuss how I came to understand why each experience was necessary in the first place. You'll also learn why it's so powerful to go from thinking your life experiences are punishing you to understanding that whatever you experience in life is happening specifically so you can change everything for the better.

Ultimately, our human experience is asking for us to be students of life. With that being the case, you'd think I would be a master of life. I have three science degrees and I own over 500 books. I spend most of my time trying to teach myself something new or traveling the world seeking out gurus who are gracious enough to take me under their wing.

In my mind, I was the embodiment of the phrase "student of life." I've always had a ferocious appetite for learning and evolving. In college, I'd sometimes read and study for 16-20 hours in a single day. But there's a huge difference between the lessons and tests we receive in the classroom versus the ones we receive in life.

In school, lessons are laid out perfectly in a nicely arranged curriculum. We're given a teacher to communicate lessons and time to prepare for the test. We even know what day the test is going to be on. In life, you don't get time to prepare nor do you get the lesson first. In life you get tested, then it's your job to figure out what the lesson was. I guess that's why they say hindsight is 20/20.

I poured my soul into this book as a form of therapy. I hope the vulnerability that comes from being completely exposed will liberate me from the fear of doing so, as well as inspire others to do the same as they seek to restore wholeness in their own lives.

We all need healing to some degree. Not one of us is perfect. If we were, we wouldn't be here. The fact that we're here means there's still work for each of us to do. Taking ownership of what needs healing is the first monumental step of any healing journey. Healing is the worthiest journey we can embark upon that has no final destination.

Too many of us are still fighting wars that are decades old. Living our lives as if everything is okay, like an old war veteran hiding the effects of post-traumatic stress. I want you to know it's okay to not be okay. You don't have to pretend like you always have it together. The reality is, things fall apart. And when they do, it's sometimes necessary to revisit old traumas before you can heal. However, it's also important to understand we can't live in the past.

At some point, we'll all come across something or someone who will knowingly or unknowingly victimize us. Part of what you'll learn in this book is "hurt people hurt people." Playing the blame game and wanting to be right doesn't lead to healing or understanding. Even when others are at fault, focusing on blame is only a distraction from healing and becoming whole again.

It doesn't matter how broken you are, anyone can be redeemed. Some of us are shattered into a thousand broken pieces. Others are simply cracked down the middle. No matter where you stand in your journey, you can use this book as a framework for restoring your oneness and seeing your life differently. Discover a new way to look at your failures that includes success. Let the lessons in this book inspire you to get unstuck and take the kind of leap of faith that sets your soul on fire.

Part I

My Story

MY

EARLY

YEARS

LITTLE BOBBY

Death was a common theme for me growing up during the late 80s and 90s amidst the crack-cocaine era. Crack cocaine was raging throughout the ghettos and suburbs, dismantling families, and pumping violence into every space it could fit. I watched it eat away at both sides of my family and saw the numbing effects it had on my friend's parents, who were reduced to zombie-like shells of themselves. I even had to watch a friend's mother prostitute herself to feed her addiction. While other kids laughed and made jokes about his heartbreak, I consoled him. That was just who I was. The soft kid at heart who everyone wanted to make hard; and eventually they did.

To give some context, according to Neighborhood Scout, it has a crime rate of 68 per 1,000 residents. One of the highest crime rates in America compared to all communities of all sizes, from the smallest towns to the very largest cities. To put this in perspective, the city of Los Angeles has a crime rate of 60 per 1,000 residents.

Growing up in the projects in my hometown, a city about an hour north of the Florida state line and a few hours south of Atlanta, was like a dangerous adventure. You had no choice but to be a part of it daily. There were all sorts of death-defying acts that were absolutely unacceptable everywhere else in the world but were normal rules of engagement for us. The frustrations of poverty, oppression, empty bellies, and broken hearts spilled out in the streets, like a busted radiator in a rundown car.

The first housing project I remember living in was Chuck's Projects. My mother, my three siblings, and I lived in a studio apartment with a kerosene heater and wash tub because it didn't have a bathtub. The place was so run down. I remember kicking a hole in the front door in frustration because I came home from school in kindergarten, and no one was there.

As a child growing up, most of the time I felt like I was in a constant state of emergency. For instance, when I was a small child around 4 or 5, I watched my mother get arrested for stealing me and my siblings food to eat. The heartbreak of seeing my mother handcuffed and taken to jail is no less painful now than it was over three decades ago. No one really asks what experiencing things like this does to a child or even an adult for that matter. Having to be a firsthand witness, I know it leaves a permanent mark that can't be erased or forgotten.

At age 7 or 8, we moved from Chuck's to the Peterson Projects. I honestly expected little to change since my mom, two sisters, my younger brother, and I had already moved around a lot after my parents got divorced. I quickly learned that this place was going to be different and that things had gone from bad to worse.

I was what you called a latchkey kid, meaning I was a child at home for long periods of time without adult supervision. And just like any young boy, I was either getting myself into trouble or trying to get myself out of it. I was a quiet kid with a big mouth so, I ended up in a lot of fights. In the hood, I figured out having a big bark wasn't enough. You had to have a matching bite to get respect. But I hated fighting. I felt horrible if I lost and even worse if I won. It seemed like I was getting into a fight almost every other day. I never understood fighting. My heart was too soft for it. And it felt like every kid in the neighborhood sensed it, like blood in the water of a shark tank.

In the late 80s and early 90s, there weren't any of these anti-bully campaigns you hear about today. It was customary for parents to send you back out into the streets if you got your ass whooped and tell you not to come home until you won the fight.

After suffering a handful of bloody noses, my father put me in Taekwondo to teach me how to defend myself. Initially, I loved everything about martial arts. After all, Bruce Lee was and still is one of my favorite human beings. But imagine me walking through the projects in full karate gear going to practice. It only made things worse by inspiring every kid I walked past to challenge me. With every challenge, I quickly found out Taekwondo didn't work in real life like it did in the movies. What worked was getting a Nintendo for Christmas.

Almost overnight this turned every fist into a friend. *Mario Brothers, Duck Hunt, Tecmo Bowl,* and Mike Tyson's *Punchout* were on virtually every commercial break on Saturdays back then, and guess who had those games in his possession?

It wasn't until I became the first kid in the projects with a Nintendo game system that other kids started gravitating towards me. I'm dating myself, but Nintendo was the predecessor of PlayStation. And playing *Mario Brothers* and *Duck Hunt* was how every kid wanted to spend every waking moment.

Now, every kid in the neighborhood was showing up on my doorstep wondering if I was home. I was never really a gamer or a people person; yet, this gaming system attracted so many random kids to my mom's door claiming to be my friend. I found myself trapped. My new "friends" were only interested in me for the opportunity to grab the Nintendo joystick.

And guess what? I hated it. I was a loner as a kid. Having a Nintendo whittled my alone time down to zero. Eventually, it became too much for me and I stopped letting people in. I put the TV and gaming system near my bedroom window and let kids play in exchange for cookies or whatever they could offer by handing the controller through the window.

I thought this would deter some of the traffic. Man, was I wrong. In a final attempt to sabotage the whole operation, I traded my Nintendo to a kid named Shawn in exchange for his Atari and 64 games I never planned to play. My mom foiled the entire plot, cursed me out, and made me go get my game system back.

My plan failed, though having that plan proved I didn't want the attention that came with having the game system. It also introduced me to Shawn and we later became friends for better or worse.

Before this, I spent much of my earlier childhood with either my cousin Donald or alone in an isolated bliss, enjoying nature and solitude. When I could, I woke up early before the rest of the neighborhood came alive. I'd disappear unbothered into either a nearby forest or a ditch. I enjoyed collecting rocks and tadpoles or hanging out in an abandoned car I found in the middle of the woods.

One day while wandering around in a ditch to collect rocks, a shadow took away my light. When I looked up it was an older kid asking me, "What the hell are you doing?"

I showed him the sack of rocks I recovered from the mud. He took a liking to one of them.

"Here, you can have it," I said giving it to him as a gift.

"Thanks. I like your shoes. What size are they?"

If you grew up in the hood you already know where this question is going. Although he was older and much bigger than me, the size of my feet was way ahead of my physical growth. My shoes were safe.

The bigger kid's name was Corey. He became the big brother I never had. He protected me when he needed to and beat me up to show me how to fight. He often instigated fights with other kids to get me some practice in "the ring."

By the time I was in the 6th grade, there was a crew of ten to twelve of us riding around on our bikes, wreaking havoc, and doing what neighborhood kids do. I wasn't the soft, good-natured kid I once was anymore. I had become what I once didn't understand. Our environments tend to do that to us.

To prove that point further, the first time I was arrested was at the tender age of 11-years-old. That certainly wasn't the last. I was arrested for vagrancy, cursing, stealing, and even running away from the cops after fighting. Most of the time the neighborhood "OG" would come get me out.

Once, my mom and siblings had to leave church and come down to the station to pick me up in their Sunday's best. One of the arresting officers just so happened to be one of my martial art instructors.

You can imagine the amount of disappointment I felt coming from all angles. Most of all, it felt like I let my little brother down. The look on his face was the look you would expect after watching your hero lose to the bad guys.

It was the first time I felt shame and a lack of self-worth. But the experience taught me the value of integrity and grew me up quickly, which was critical for what was going to happen to me over the next couple of years.

CHANGING COURSE

A new school year ushered in a new era of life for me. I had a new set of influences. I experienced growing pains of epic proportions. It felt as if things were slowly spiraling out of control before I could grasp what was happening or brace myself for the aftermath.

I was suspended from regular school for six months just because I snatched my arm from my teacher during recess. To provide some background, in 7th grade I sprouted up to 6 feet and weighed about 175 pounds. And at my school, it was common to see full-out brawls before, during, and especially after school. The reasons would range from accidentally bumping into the wrong person or stepping on someone's Air Jordans. To be honest, most of the reasons we would mangle each other were silly. But this is exactly what kept everyone on edge and ready to strike.

While out at recess, my teacher came to simply grab me and bring me inside after taking too long. I snatched my arm ready to fight because there was a brewing beef I was a part of earlier that day. I thought the grab might be from one of those kids. I quickly apologized, but it was too late.

After serving my six months of in-school suspension, the principal told me I could return to my classes after I apologized to the teacher.

When I arrived in his office, I saw the teacher involved and her husband. She told me how traumatic the experience was for her and how it made her have nightmares and have to see a therapist. Her husband told me that if I was older, he'd kick my ass.

I empathized with her because I never wanted a woman to be afraid of me. I was the protector of my three sisters and my mom. So, I understood how the husband felt.

I let them both vent uninterrupted. The whole time, all I could think about was the dead body me and my cousin Donald found wandering in the woods, all the times I heard gunshots ring out while playing basketball, and all the fights I'd witnessed or been a part of already that year.

The life I was forced to endure compared to the life my teacher and her husband lived were as close as Jupiter is to Mars. The boy I was out in the world and the boy I was inside were in constant conflict. Because of my crazy growth spurt, now standing at 6 feet and 175 pounds, I wasn't the pushover who got bullied when I was younger.

LOSS OF INNOCENCE

When it came to violence, by the time I was 13, I was ready for anything that came my way. I had seen and experienced so much already, and had become a willing participant, especially with fighting.

By the end of 7th grade, my life spiraled into a violent rage. Even today, as I think back on that time of my life, most of the things that happened to me, I had forgotten about. Probably in an attempt to suppress the need to deal with the trauma of it all.

That same year, I witnessed my friend, Corey, brutally murder another one of my friends using a bat during an altercation. I can still remember my five-mile walk home… numb…in a zombie-like state after witnessing the violent murder. I kept asking myself, "Was it real? Was he really dead?

What was going to happen to Corey?" I wanted to believe I'd wake up and realize it was just a bad dream.

No child should have to see or experience that. Even Corey was a child. Nobody won that day. I lost two friends and more of my innocence, and two families lost their children in different ways. I spent the next years of my life having nightmares about what happened. The thud from the bat still rings in my ears from time-to-time. I checked out emotionally that day and it would be a decade before I would allow myself to have another meaningful relationship.

Without Corey around, I felt unprotected. All I had left was my cousin, Donald. Most of my other friends were going to jail or doing things I wouldn't even do. To cope I acted out, dealt drugs or participated in violence.

Although he was older, Donald looked up to me like a big brother. He asked me to get him a gun because he was being bullied when I wasn't around. I did. I don't even remember where I got it from. I had my own gun at the time and true enough he was being bullied sometimes; so, I wanted to protect him. It never occurred to me he could get into trouble with it.

Had I understood at 13 that giving him a gun to protect himself by scaring someone with it was dangerous, I never would have.

Then again, we'd witnessed robberies, drug deals, dead bodies, and gunshots being fired around my hood like regularly scheduled TV programming in the 90s. Where I grew up, no one liked to go home at night because that's when things got worse. It was like being part of a reality show without the cameras. No one wanted to miss out on a second of the entertainment because it was so action packed.

In the wee hours of the night, the whole hood stood on corners set against each other, waiting for the next epic moment to pop off. Sometimes when things got boring, we instigated friction where there was none. So, giving Donald the gun was equivalent to bringing a coat out on a Friday night in September to watch high school football. It's better to have it and not need it, than to need it and not have it.

A few months later, Donald went missing. There were a few times Donald left home and came to hideout with me, and my father would call looking for him. Donald being 'missing' wasn't unusual. But when my father called me looking for him and he wasn't with me, I grew afraid.

A few days later, my father identified his body at the morgue.

Donald was killed in a car chase with the police. He and some other kids had stolen a car. While attempting to elude the police, they crashed into a semi-truck. Only my cousin was killed.

The morning my father walked in and told me, "Donald is dead," something broke in me I'm not sure will ever be fixed. If there was any innocence left in me, I lost it that day. The crew that was once ten or twelve had dwindled down to two or three in violent fashion.

I blame myself for what happened to him because I wasn't being a good influence, even though I tried to hide the things I was doing. I blamed his mother because of her drug addiction. I blamed the other kids he was with because they knew me and should've told me he was figuratively in the wrong lane. I blamed the police for chasing them. But most of the weight I put on myself.

A year after it happened, I had a vivid dream. It was late at night and Donald knocked on my front door. It wasn't typical because he usually came to the window of my room. My younger sister answered the door and told me he was there. When I came to the door, he was smiling. I walked outside and we hugged. He told me, "It wasn't your fault. It was just my time. You and I agreed upon it before we came here in this life. It was hard living this life, but I'm glad I did it for you."

"How am I supposed to go on without you?" I asked him. "You were the only true friend I had. We always dreamed and made plans to get out of the hood together, go to college, and live on the same street."

"You won't be without me. I'll be with you until you come home."

After he said that, he hugged me and walked away into the darkness, in the direction of the graveyard next to the projects I lived in. That's the only dream I've had of him. It was heavy for me at 13 just as it is still heavy for me as an adult. Through that dream which felt surreal, I was able to finally make my peace with his death. Later I found out the gun I gave him was taken the next day after I gave it to him.

AN ODE TO DONALD

Before meeting Corey, the only person I considered a friend and my only true friend was my cousin, Donald. It's still very painful for me to talk about him. He was more than my cousin and best friend; he was more like a brother to me. We were what the old folks would call frick and frack. He was kind-hearted. He wouldn't swat a fly.

Donald was my first cousin. My father's nephew. He lived with my grandmother because my aunt, his mom, was struggling with drug addiction. She was so beautiful; but, drugs turned her into the walking dead.

We stayed at my father's almost every weekend. As a younger child, I had severe asthma that would sometimes hospitalize me. I'd experience these bouts of asthmatic pneumonia where I could barely breathe and often thought I would die, panting throughout the night and wheezing, trying to catch a breath.

I remember Donald would be afraid to go to sleep because sometimes I would stop breathing. Whenever this happened, he'd wake me up or pat my chest repeatedly like my father would do to help break up the mucus in my lungs. I don't think I've let anyone get that close to me since he died. He was a good soul. In many ways, I believe he was my soulmate (without the romantic connotation that most people associate with soulmates) or soul brothers with soul ties.

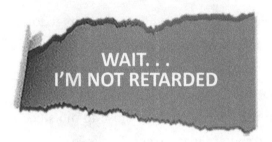

WAIT. . .
I'M NOT RETARDED

The next year, I dragged myself into eighth grade trying to pick up the pieces and stitch myself together emotionally. The one thing I still had on my side was, although I had a propensity for the wrong crowd and violence, I always made good grades. I thought maybe I should start there.

On the first day of school, I noticed the kids in my class had changed dramatically. Most of the kids in my class now were the troublemakers and a few of them were what I thought of at the time (mind of a 13-year-old) as "slow."

The teacher asked us to crack open our books to start the lesson. She then asked the class one question from the book. "If Sally has 4 seashells and Johnny has 9 seashells and she gives Johnny 2 of them, how many seashells does Johnny now have?"

I knew I was in the wrong place. *Simple arithmetic in 8th grade? How did I progress to the 8th grade but was learning backward?* I thought.

I raised my hand and asked the teacher, "Am I in the retarded class?"

The class laughed; I didn't. I knew something was wrong. I just didn't know how to communicate it.

"Stop disrupting class," she snapped.

She hadn't answered my question.

I asked again. "Am I in the retarded class?"

Instead of answering me, she threatened, "I'm going to send you to the principal's office if you have another outburst."

I got up, left the classroom, and headed straight to the principal's office. When I saw him sitting at his desk, I asked, "Why have I been placed in the retarded class? I don't understand because I've always gotten good grades."

I honestly thought it was a mistake.

"Bobby, please go back to class." He responded without looking up from the papers on his desk.

I refused.

"What do I need to do to get out of that class because I don't belong there?"

I guess after he saw I would not give up, he finally gave me his attention and answered. "The only way you can get out of that class is if your mother signs a waiver to get you out."

I called my mother.

When she arrived, he attempted to convince her to keep me in the remedial class. My mother almost agreed with him; but, I was so adamant she finally sided with me instead. After signing the waiver, my mom left. The principal walked me to my new class. He tapped on the classroom door and opened it, interrupting the teacher mid-lesson to introduce me as a new student.

She looked stunned.

"I'd like to speak with you both outside," she said, looking at me puzzled.

"Have you taken pre-algebra before?" she asked me.

"No," I answered truthfully.

She looked at the principal as if she wanted to wring his neck. "Why would you put him in a class he doesn't have the prerequisite classes for?"

"Because there are no more classes available."

At that point, she focused all her attention on me. "Are you going to be any trouble?"

I quickly answered, "No."

"It's going to be very difficult for you to do well without having taken pre-algebra because this is an advanced placement class."

"I will sit in the front row if you want me to, and I'll never be late to class or with assignments."

At the end of the semester, I finished the class with an A. When my teacher handed me my final test back, she asked me to stay after class because she wanted to talk to me.

Once everyone left, this stern, no-nonsense white woman teared up and hugged me. I honestly didn't know what to do because I hadn't seen one ounce of emotion come from her before that day.

After she hugged me, she looked straight into my eyes saying, "You were put in this class to fail just like you were put in the educatable retarded class to fail. Not everybody is going to believe in you but that doesn't matter because you do. You can do whatever you want to do. I'm so proud of you."

I never forgot that moment. I'm so proud of the 13-year-old version of myself, fighting for something better than accepting the box society wanted to throw me in.

As I think back, I realized I was put into that class like many other students because we were perceived as violent, uneducable, and a waste of time. No one ever asked if I was okay or if I needed to speak to someone. If they had, any decent human being would've understood what I had gone through the prior year was enough to give even an adult PTSD.

However, it was outside my control. What was in my control was how I responded to whatever life gave me. I decided I wanted more and deserved more. Nothing was going to stop me.

My Early Years in Retrospect: Sifting for the Lessons

Whenever I tell someone I grew up in the projects, I often see a slight look of disbelief spread across their face. I don't think it's because I'm a doctor or because I'm articulate. The look of disbelief comes from their inability to fathom where I came from versus where I am today. For them, the gap seems much too wide. They can't begin to imagine what life experiences could've possibly occurred to cover that amount of distance for one human being.

The odds were definitely stacked against me from the start. Thankfully, I had an inner resolve not to allow others to dictate to me what I was "supposed" to be (a failure) based on circumstances outside of my control. I had to learn early in life that I could rewrite my story in my favor and be a winner in life, no matter what. I became the author of my own story and never looked back. Until now.

By the time I was 13-years-old, I had to experience my best friend/cousin being killed, witness my closest non-relative friend brutally beat another childhood friend to death with a bat, and had another friend get life in prison because of a robbery turned homicide.

As a man today, almost 30 years later, the death of my cousin Donald is still my greatest trauma and where I feel the greatest amount of survivor's guilt. I feel guilty, not for the gun itself, because it got taken from him before it was never used. The guilt came from believing I put the mentality in his mind that ultimately led him to do something he or I would've never done. He was far more susceptible to peer pressure than I was. I wasn't the influence I should've been for him which is what ultimately led to his demise. It's taken me years to forgive my 13-year-old self.

Periods of being Little Bobby revealed a version of me I've hated and disowned almost all my life. Through therapy, relentless self-evaluation, and courage to be vulnerable, I finally forgave myself. And when I did, I let out a cry so loud and carefree it could've touched the souls of anyone within a thirty-block radius. The whole time I was crying, I had the vision of me as an adult and Donald embracing the 13-year-old version of me crying uncontrollably.

I've never done anything more liberating. I never knew how shackled this trauma kept me until I released it.

My love, heart, and soul are different now. It took me a while to realize I shutdown and turned off emotionally when he passed away. That impacted the depth of every relationship I've had moving forward. I never allowed myself to fully love anyone because I was no longer capable of loving myself. I didn't believe I deserved love because of the guilt. I never considered that I was only a child or valued that I had become a different person. By taking all that into perspective, I understand today why Donald told me it wasn't my fault in the dream.

We can only operate at the level of consciousness we're at when things happen. However, it is our job to grow from those experiences and become higher versions of ourselves. Forgiveness and patience with myself have been the perfect prescription for my healing process. I learned a lot about loss through my early experiences and how to pick up the pieces when things fall apart. Most importantly, I learned the lesson of forgiveness. The importance of forgiving myself first, and secondly, the importance of forgiving others to let go of unhealthy attachments.

It can be gut-wrenching to do an inventory of all the traumas we've experienced in our lives.

Society is always creating boxes for us to fit nicely and quietly into. These boxes aren't determined by what you're capable of, but by who they believe you are. This is why it's so important to "Know Thyself."

Because when you know who you are, you'll at the very least know what you don't want. This is only half the battle. Knowing what you don't want is critical when ending up somewhere you don't want to be. Like when I landed in the remedial class. I didn't know how to articulate what I was feeling, but I knew there was a bigger plan for me.

Another very important lesson I learned is we are all just a microcosm of the experiences our environment creates. When it's difficult to change how you feel on the inside, change your external environment. Change your friends, where you go, what you do, the interior of your room or home, and even your classroom if you have to (like I did).

It's often the people we love and look up to the most that put us in boxes too small for what's inside of us. They do it out of what they believe is love. They believe they're protecting us. Ultimately, they're only projecting their own self-limiting beliefs onto us.

Take time to self-reflect. Ask yourself what traumas haven't you healed from? Where is it in your life that you need to forgive yourself for things you've inappropriately blamed yourself for? We blame ourselves for being molested, poor, and bullied. And when we do, we often never fully recover until we embrace forgiveness of ourselves first and acceptance of the reality that it happened. Ultimately, it's our job to heal from it.

Even today when reflecting on my own journey, I often ask myself if many of the things I experienced actually happened. I guess what makes them questionable is I don't believe my shoulders are broad enough today to bear those types of experiences again. Whatever happens to us in our lives is because we are perfectly suited to play the cards we are dealt.

MY

YOUNG ADULT

YEARS

SOUL FOOD MEMORIES

My fondest memories of food growing up were family gatherings at my grandparents' home. My grandmother was the kind of cook whose food was so good, you always wondered why she wouldn't open a restaurant of her own. I watched her cook without using measuring tools or recipes. A pinch of this, two punches of that, then taste it to make sure it's just right.

The aromas were intoxicating enough to make you feel euphoric if you were in the room and strong enough for cars passing by to know dinner was on the stove. My grandmother looked like a mad scientist in the kitchen. I loved her cooking so much that I thought it was the result of magic. I'd take a seat at the table to see if sparks were flying or at least some form of sorcery to explain what made her food so addictive.

Every holiday, food flooded the tables so much we all had to eat seated on couches or standing up. Nobody ever complained. We ate, smiled, laughed and joked about how fast we all ate and how often we went back for seconds and thirds.

My family felt like the real-life version of the movie *Soul Food*. My 'Big Mama' Lily Pearl made food so tantalizing it would squash quarrels between family members you thought were unforgivable. I loved my grandmother so deeply. I can vividly remember praying to God for her when I was eight. During one of my grandfather's bible study sessions, I asked God not to take her away before I died.

My grandfather was an entirely different story. He was a strong, proud man who ruled with an iron fist. Most of my family members said very few words to my grandfather. He didn't play games and he was very tight with his wallet. Despite all this, I liked to make him smile. I'd do things like sit in his chair that everyone else knew was off limits.

I would see him coming in the door and run to sit in it. He wore a scowl on his face that seemed permanent, but when he saw me sitting in his chair, he would crack a barely noticeable smile and signal for me to get up. One day, I went so far as to sit in his lap after he plopped down in his chair. It was the most intimate experience I had with him or had seen anyone else have with him.

He was the first to be stricken with diabetes.

As his health deteriorated, diabetes began picking him away like a sniper on the roof: high blood sugar, elevated blood pressure, blurred vision, and amputation. Ultimately, a heart attack took his life.

It was my first confrontation with the ruthlessness of chronic disease, but not my last.

I watched my paternal grandmother go through the same slow death as my maternal grandfather. Watching both of them die, I feared for my maternal grandmother's life. She seemed too young and too good for the world to die. I wanted her to be around until I became someone special, so she could be proud of me. But not long after my grandfather passed away, she became ill. She was diagnosed with colorectal cancer.

Although the news struck fear in my heart, I truly believed she was too much of an angel to die. She was the epitome of a good soul. I watched her give her last, break her back, and take food off her own plate to feed anyone who showed up at the door hungry (I watched my mom do the same). Most importantly, I needed her. By age 15, my entire world had been flipped upside down. I wanted to know she'd be there to assure me everything was going to be alright.

To cope with everything that was happening as a teenager, I found my solace in sports. I became known as the "boy with the ball" because I dribbled my basketball all over the city. It was the therapy I didn't know I needed at the time. I practiced into the wee hours of the night. Even after the streetlights went out and the rim was barely visible. It was often so dark; the sound of the net was the only way to could confirm I made a shot.

I'll never forget the call. I received an urgent call from my cousin while at basketball camp. My grandmother was on her deathbed and she wanted me there at her side. My heart sank to the bottom of my belly after hanging up.

When I arrived at her home, everyone was in a somber mood. She was both the glue and the fabric that held our family together. I made my way through the river of tears, blank stares, and the trail of broken hearts to see her. When I made it to her room, I stopped at the door and saw her surrounded by my immediate family. I realized the hospital sent her home to die. The mere thought of that crushed any hope I had for a miracle.

As I walked up to her bedside, my family made room for me to be next to her. I grabbed her hand and held it as tight as I could to feel the life she still had in her body. She clutched my hand in return and stared at the ceiling, wheezing to catch her breath.

"I made it, Grandma. I'm here. I love you so much. You mean the world to me. But, it's okay to let go."

At that admission, I sat there. Still clutching her hand, I cried like a baby. After some time passed, when her grip loosened, I left the room. Midway down the hall, I paused in my tracks as the entire room erupted in tears and loud sobs. She was gone.

At only 15, all my grandparents were deceased because of some form of chronic illness. I made a vow that I was going to become a healer and change people's lives using health as my weapon against disease.

COLLEGE BOUND

A few months after my grandmother passed, during a routine checkup to play sports, my doctor diagnosed me with high blood pressure. I couldn't believe it. I was an athlete, physically fit, and only had about 7% body fat.

Death and disease seemed like a monkey on my back that wouldn't be satisfied until I was in the ground. Only, I was now numb to the thought of death. I swept my diagnosis under the rug to keep from falling apart. I convinced myself it was just a combination of bad genes and misfortune.

My grandmother's death and the hypertension diagnosis weighed heavily on me. I felt lost and empty. She was the glue in our family and the center of my heart. I wanted to take the time to grieve her, but I didn't get the chance. Before I could begin to process everything, I found out my girlfriend at the time was pregnant with my son.

It felt like my whole life was falling apart at the seams. I was just a baby about to have a baby because I was trying to play an adult. My fantasies of hoop dreams and getting out of the hood faded and a dark reality settled in.

Until that point and despite everything I had already survived, I'd always had a vivid imagination about what was possible for me. Suddenly, all I could envision was me finding a "good" job at a local factory or maybe being lucky enough to get a scholarship at a small school.

It was too difficult to articulate how I felt and far too painful to face reality. So, I did what I always did when there were no answers and nowhere to turn. I found my solace in playing basketball into the twilight hours of the night, listening to Tupac. The basketball court was the one place I could still dream, and playing basketball was the only thing that gave me joy at the time. It was the perfect escape from the shock I was going through.

The idea of getting someone pregnant never crossed my adolescent mind. Somehow, it became all I could think about. How was I going to be someone's father? I was just a stupid little kid myself. After all I had been through, this felt like it was going to be the straw that broke the camel's back. At the time, it felt like my life was over.

I was getting meaner by the day and my threshold for what I was willing to do to prove a point had exceeded the boundaries of normal rationale. Unattended hurt and grief will always spill out in violence in some shape or form eventually. I was a walking time bomb. So, I guess life intervened to keep me from imploding.

The birth of my son extinguished a few internal fires and grounded me which gave me enough time to unclench my fists and discover I was pretty smart in chemistry and anatomy.

Throughout high school, I hid how smart I was by never taking books home or answering questions in class. Still, my teachers and coaches quickly took notice when I started applying myself. I didn't need anybody to tell me I was smart. I'd already convinced myself of that fact. But challenging myself academically helped me discover that there was another way out. I didn't want to depend on some random college coach deciding whether or not to give me a scholarship. I liked the idea of controlling my own destiny better, so I put more of my focus on academics.

I managed to get through high school. After graduating, I started college in Atlanta at Georgia State University. However, it still felt like I had one foot out and one foot in the ghetto.

NO TURNING BACK

After finally getting into college and making the basketball team, I thought I would spend the rest of my life accomplishing my dreams. Like countless others, I struggled in so many ways my freshman year.

I had never been on a college campus. I wasn't even aware I needed to register for classes, sign up for the dorms, or declare a major. I also struggled socially. Even though there were a substantial amount of other African-American students on campus, they were nothing like me. They seemed to fit perfectly into the puzzle of college life. They were joining fraternities, picking majors, and partying like it was 1999. They drove "Daddy's" Lexus on the weekends and bragged about family connections that would afford them summer internships.

On many levels, I resented them for having it so easy. Since I was still rough around the edges with a hood mentality, I embraced the underdog position. I worked more. I studied more and partied less. Sometimes, I'd study until midnight in a nearby Barnes & Noble. Seeing my classmates dressed to impress walking by on their way to clubs never bothered me though. I had too much to lose. It actually made it easy to keep the eye of the tiger and never take my eye off the prize. I studied as much as 8 to 10 hours a day, then went to work for another 8 hours.

After my freshman year, I returned home for the summer feeling proud and on top of the world for successfully finishing the year. When I arrived in town, I found out my younger brother had been beaten up and had suffered a black eye. Infuriated, I threw him in the car, picked up two friends and went on a manhunt.

When we finally found the people responsible, I pulled up and jumped out of the car. I told my brother to point out who had put their hands on him.

One of my friends saw I was in a rage and outnumbered, so he gave me a gun. While my brother was pointing out what seemed to be a full dozen guys, one of them charged me. I pulled out the gun, hit him across the head with it and we tussled against a car. In the middle of the struggle, another person broke a bottle across the back of my head. I knocked him away, then picked the guy I was fighting with up over my head. For a moment everyone stopped and just watched.

I saw a nearby parking stomp and decided I was going to throw him down onto it. But in the process, he grabbed the back of my shirt, and instead I hit the pavement headfirst breaking my neck. Once I shook myself out of the daze, I realized I still had the gun in my hand. I cocked it, put it to his stomach, and pulled the trigger. Nothing. I punched back a few more times, cocked it again, and pulled the trigger. Nothing. So, I tossed the gun. The same friend who gave it to me, picked it up, shot in the air four times and everybody scattered.

By this time, you could hear police sirens in the distance. I jumped in the car with my brother and pulled off. It wasn't until we were about a mile away and the adrenaline faded that I realized there was something seriously wrong with my neck. I ended up almost crashing the car.

I drove to a nearby hospital. After seeing the on-call physician in the emergency room, she told me a few of the vertebrae in my neck were cracked. She chastised and berated me for my foolishness. The whole time all I could think about was, *Why didn't the gun work when I pulled the trigger? What if it did?* I realized I had pulled myself out of the mud only to jump right back into it. I was taking every blessing God gave me and throwing it in the trash to make sure I was still upholding hood politics.

The next day, broken neck and all, I drove three hours back to my university and enrolled in summer school. I struggled the entire drive back. And I struggled the entire summer in class with a neck brace on. But that's ok, I was free. The gun jamming was a second chance. If it hadn't jammed, I would've been spending the rest of my life in prison.

It made me realize that I learned things growing up in the hood that were no longer applicable to where I was and where I wanted to go in life. I had to unlearn everything I knew and instead focus on navigating my new world to stand a chance of going any further. Unlearning was going to be just as important to my future as learning was.

AGAINST ALL ODDS

In the last semester of my senior year at Georgia State, I took 23 credit hours of all chemistry and math courses while working a work-study job at school and another job at a hospital. After graduating undergrad with two science degrees, I felt like the American dream. I thought the world of opportunities would come pouring in. The life of struggle I once knew was just a thing of the past.

Initially, I was headed to medical school; so, I decided to move to the New York area. I started working in a hospital while studying for the MCAT to get into medical school.

A few of the physicians at the hospital took me under their wings. One of the surgeons would grab me to help him anytime he was there, and a General Practitioner named Dr. Ye quizzed me constantly. He even allowed me to collect blood samples from patients and insert their catheters to get practical experience.

However, things didn't go as well as I would've hoped, even though I did fine on the MCAT. So, I moved back to Atlanta with a friend who graciously offered me his couch until I got on my feet. After about two months of being there, he told me he was moving in with his cousin and I'd need to find my own place.

I had too much pride at the time to tell him I didn't have the money or the means to do that. When it came time to leave, I can remember taking the last of my things to my car thinking, *How did I get to this place? I'm a hard worker and I'm educated. How did this happen?*

On the last trip back to my car, a homeless guy sitting in an alley, interrupted my mental daze by asking me for money. Hearing him ask me for money made me realize I was now homeless, too. It upset me to come to that realization. So much that I screamed at him, "I don't have any damn money. I'm homeless just like you!"

A look of pity spread across his face. Then, he reached in his bag and grabbed a pack of cookies and offered them to me. I fell to my knees in tears. He consoled me. I sat with him in the dead of winter for the rest of the night.

I asked how he ended up on the streets before explaining what happened to me. He started teaching me the tricks of being homeless. He explained how to keep warm, legal ways to get money, places to get free food, and shelters that would take men in.

I appreciate every moment we spent together. At the same time, I resented it. I didn't want to get comfortable being homeless. I intentionally made myself as uncomfortable as possible. After 34 days of sleeping in my car, I got three jobs. One was an overnight position, so I didn't have to worry about being cold or sleeping outside. I also got a gym membership for $29 so I could take showers. My goal was to work myself out of homelessness.

One day out of the blue, my friend Johnny called telling me he was coming to town and wanted to stay with me. I told him I was looking for a new place to stay. I didn't tell him the truth. That I'd been sleeping in my car for months. He suggested I stay with his cousin Travis who had an extra room.

Travis and I were cool. He had been like a big brother to me in college. I called to ask if he had a spare room for me. He told me to come by and check it out. I put $20 worth of gas in my car, that had become a mobile home, and drove over to his place the same day. He had no idea I'd been praying for something like this to happen or that I had everything I owned in my car, ready to move in.

I walked in and caught up with him for a moment. After checking out the room as if I had other options, I asked if it was okay for me to grab a few things and move in that night. He said it was cool. I went out to my car and just thanked God for about two hours. Then, started unloading my things.

Five months later, after a lot of hours worked and learning everything I could about real estate, I purchased my first home. A few months after that I bought two additional rental properties. In less than a year's time, I had gone from homeless to landlord.

At 25, having two rental properties and my own home felt like a fairy tale. Hurricane Katrina had just devastated New Orleans and Atlanta became a safe haven for many of the displaced residents. So, I rented out one home to a family that escaped New Orleans just in time. Things were going great.

One weekend while heading back to Atlanta after a trip to New York, a fork in the road presented a totally new direction for me. Right before takeoff, I took a call from my mortgage broker to discuss a deal I had on the table. The woman sitting next to me must have been ear hustling because she asked me a thousand questions about investing in real estate.

After answering the barrage of questions, I asked her what she did for a living. She told me she was a pharmacist. I knew what a pharmacist was, but had no idea what they did behind the counter at the pharmacy. She explained what her job involved and other opportunities possible in the field of pharmacy, which intrigued me.

Every science had a special place in my heart, but chemistry even more so. The idea of marrying chemistry with healthcare seemed like a really dope idea. Instead of closing a real estate deal when I got back to Atlanta, I decided to look into pharmacy school.

I scheduled a visit with a pharmacy school in Atlanta and sent them my transcripts to see if it was a better fit for me than medical school. By the time the visit was over, I was as convinced as the people I met with that it was a perfect fit. A few months later, I went back to interview and was quickly accepted.

In the meantime, I was teaching friends how to buy properties, renovate them, and acquire tenants. One morning, I received a frantic call from a friend saying his mortgage payments had almost doubled from his initial payment. I told him to call the bank and I would make my way over to help him figure out what his next move would be.

Upon reviewing his closing documents, I saw he had what was called an adjustable-rate mortgage. This meant that the first few months of the loan would be lower payments and without warning, the rate would adjust, thereby adjusting the mortgage payment. This particular friend had purchased six houses in the last two years. I read through all of his paperwork and discovered all of his payments were about to skyrocket.

I ran home to check my paperwork and noticed I was sitting in the same boat he was. This period would later become known as the mortgage crisis.

The next day, I called my ex-girlfriend and asked if she had any preference on which house I should keep. Everything else was put on the market. I was fortunate enough to sell all of them except the one I lived in and one rental property. I let the tenant know what was going on and gave them free rent and moving expenses to help them transition.

Now, all I could think about was potentially having a foreclosure on my credit for the next seven years. I reached out to a couple of friends and learned there were a few ways to avoid it by reaching out to the mortgage company. When I finally spoke to someone at the bank explaining the potential error, they gave me the runaround. I even thought about filing bankruptcy to stop the foreclosure. I realized how much of a toll the stress was taking on me and my focus on pharmacy school, so I let go and stop worrying. After all, despite everything, I still felt blessed.

By this time, I had already decided I was going to pharmacy school. I was just waiting for school to start a few months later so I could go into the next phase of my life.

One day my ex-girlfriend asked me, "Would you consider buying real estate investment property again?"

Without hesitating I answered, "Absolutely!"

She looked at me almost confused. "Why? You failed miserably at it."

"Actually, I was very successful. I secured a home for myself after being homeless. I created a real estate investment program that made me $50,000. I built relationships and learned a lifetime of knowledge around buying and selling real estate," I explained to her.

The ultimate icing on the cake was the mortgage company that had my home loan, Washington Mutual Bank, ended up going bankrupt and dissolving because of fraudulent activity and the real estate crash in 2007. As a result, the home I owned that was being foreclosed on was simply returned to the bank and the foreclosure was removed from my credit files.

Sifting for the Lessons
Invisible Growth

By the age of 15, all my grandparents were deceased because of some form of chronic illness. I was diagnosed with high blood pressure, despite being an athlete and in great shape. It's also the year I became a father.

In retrospect, having my son at 15 probably saved my life. It forced me to grow up fast from a very practical perspective. A lot of the growth happening during these years was going on inside of me.

Everyone wants to eat the fruit and throw away the seed. Not realizing the seed within is what's capable of mass-producing and multiplying itself infinitely. There is a special seed planted in all of our hearts just looking for fertile ground to plant its roots. Just remember we don't grow like Amazon Prime. We grow more like bamboo.

A seed grows in the soil surrounded by darkness. In the first three years of growing a bamboo tree, you may not even see a sprout, but below the surface it is taking root and nourishing itself. In a matter of three weeks, it can grow 90 feet tall. The question is, did it grow 90 feet in three years or three weeks? The answer is both. A portion of growth is invisible to the human eye because it's internal. Likewise, there's growth we can visibly see. Be an active participant in both.

During my period of homelessness, I learned a lot about who I was as a man and what I was capable of when I got focused. I also learned a precious lesson about asking for help. Most of the people who know me have never heard this story. I was too prideful to ask them for help and too embarrassed to tell them what I was going through at the time.

To all the men out there trying to be the superman for their families, it's okay to ask for help. To all the women who are shouldering far more than they can bear, it's okay not to be okay. I had to learn the hard way, but I learned.

When I experienced my rise and ultimate fall in real estate, I learned that karma has a way of settling your disputes in a way you never could. This was a huge lesson in trust and allowing the goodness in life to work its magic. It was also a huge lesson in the importance of integrity. This is where I developed my savviness as an entrepreneur.

During this time, I was also open to receive new direction on what path I should take next. I stayed flexible to the inevitable changes, twists, and turns life presented to help me continue to evolve and learn the lessons it was teaching me.

MY

SHIFT

YEARS

BECOMING MY OWN HERO

While attending pharmacy school, I kept that same 'eye of the tiger' energy from undergrad. Although I'd come a long way, my race was a marathon. Despite everything I had accomplished, it still felt like I had one foot in and one foot out of a successful life.

When I finally walked the stage from graduate school, it was the first time I allowed myself to exhale. Not on graduation day, but on the day I finally received my diploma. It felt like a war had ended and I was a soldier without a battle to fight. I was ready to change the world. I had worked for the FDA while studying as a graduate student and had moved on to a local hospital and as a community pharmacist.

Initially, my plan was to own my own pharmacy and become a millionaire. I remember telling myself that I'd never have to worry about moving back to the hood again. That was the greatest joy of me graduating. For years, I had three degrees I never framed because it was never about status or validation. I just wanted to make my son proud and keep the promise I made to my grandmother before she died.

However, the battle of disease in my own body that I'd been distracted from while trying to survive became a new fight I'd have to win as well. Over the course of the last decade-plus, going from high school and undergrad to graduate school, my blood pressure got worse along with my overall health.

Forced to finally look at my health from a bird's-eye view, I saw it wasn't just hypertension. I had inflammation in just about every joint, suffered from sleep apnea, had gained fifty pounds since my freshman year of college, experienced chronic fatigue, and consistently had migraines. I was falling apart right before my own eyes, just like my grandfather. It was something about that moment of clarity that scared me straight into action.

Although I was a healthcare professional, the *thought* of getting my blood pressure checked elevated my blood pressure even more. Me and my physician had candid conversations around the importance of keeping my blood pressure down and taking my medication (which, of course, he knew I was aware of).

One day, I had an epiphany that changed my life forever.

I thought to myself, *How the hell am I going to help or save anyone else's life if I can't even save my own?*

I had vowed to become a healer. Instead, I had become the sick, even as a pharmacist working in a hospital.

I tried just about every diet and diet plan there was: Atkins, DASH, Mediterranean, Paleo, Keto, and all types of frozen meal delivery programs. I would lose a little weight, feel a little better, but end up returning to my old habits and gain back the weight I lost plus a few extra pounds. I even tried just about every variation of exercise you can imagine. It definitely improved my fitness, but not much of anything else changed or improved with my overall health.

Now before all of this, I knew I didn't eat healthy. I didn't have one standard or restriction for my food choices unless you counted "must be tasty" as a requirement. I didn't eat pork but that was about it. I figured any minor additional improvements would create some major changes. But nothing, zero, zilch. The younger me always thought one day I'd get older, then finally change my diet and miraculously reclaim my health. You can imagine how hopeless I felt after going through all that effort and not getting any results.

Out of sheer desperation and with a lot of apprehension, I decided to try a plant-based lifestyle as a last resort. The idea of removing meat from just one meal seemed farfetched. Let alone removing all meat, dairy, eggs, and processed foods from my diet. After all, I was used to eating some form of meat or animal product with just about every meal. I grew up eating soul food for breakfast, lunch, and dinner. And my mother was surgical in the kitchen as if my grandmother left her cooking skills as an inheritance. In my mind, a meal was incomplete without some form of meat.

However, I was desperate and at the end of my rope.

While listening to an old Tony Robbins lecture, he spoke about one point in his life when he removed animal-based products from his diet because they clogged instead of cleansed his body. So instead, he focused on green smoothies and green juices. As a result, his energy went through the roof, he eliminated inflammation, slept like a baby, and looked younger.

What did I have to lose other than weight and countless health benefits to gain? He always said it takes 21 days to change a habit. I decided I'd give it three weeks. By day 17, I had lost 21 pounds. I felt like I was walking around with an IV of Red Bull fueling me. I pushed it to 30 days. Then 60 days became 90. By the end of the 90 days, my blood pressure had gone from an average of 157/90 to 116/70. I hadn't seen my blood pressure this normal since I was 15, before my grandmother died, which was before I was diagnosed with hypertension.

I figured if these were the only benefits I'd receive, I'd be a happy man. My patients now noticed I had a new visible neckline, my white coat was now slouching off my body, my skin was vibrant, my mood was always cheerful, and I looked ten years younger. I also noticed the sleep apnea had resolved itself. All the aches in my joints had disappeared, the mental fog cleared with crystal clear clarity, and I lost 45 pounds. I looked and felt like a new man. My girlfriend at the time also noticed several improvements in the bedroom that I won't go into detail about.

Men often think they're King Kong in the bedroom when they're just a chimpanzee. Thankfully, women are sensitive and kind enough to protect our egos. Upon hearing that our intimacy was like sleeping with an updated 2.0 version of me, I was sold. And I finally realized that health isn't something you can buy or negotiate with. It's something you must earn.

Going plant-based and sticking to it was the beginning of a new era for me.

BEING THE AUTHOR OF MY OWN STORY

Adopting a whole foods plant-based lifestyle (WFPB) and incorporating herbs for detoxification, I ended up completely healing my body and changing my mind.

After I regained my health and got an ocean full of clarity, I wasn't sure I wanted to continue the career path I was on anymore. One day, I called my supervisor and told him I was going to be firing my job in two months. The next thing I know, they called me to the corporate office to speak to my boss's boss.

He told me I was a star in the company and wanted to know what he could do to keep me. My response was straight up, "I want to travel and live abroad." He told me there were opportunities abroad within the company and he could promise me I could do that in four to five years. I walked out even more convinced I was going to be quitting.

I had a newfound sense of self-value and self-worth which didn't require four to five years to figure it out on my own. I quit that job and did some soul searching for about six months. I practiced yoga, trained for races, read, traveled, and sat on the porch dreaming of possibilities.

One day while lying in the park, I got a call from a physician's office that wanted to hire me. I went in for an interview and loved the physician who owned the company. He agreed to let me make formulary decisions, counsel sick employees, and do a lot of other cool stuff. I could even take a vacation anytime I wanted. I figured, why the hell not?

A year after working with him, I was interviewed to be in a commercial for my pharmacy school and invited to be the keynote speaker at a white coat ceremony. That same year, I was also awarded "The Most Innovative Pharmacist" in Georgia. During the awards ceremony, a pharmacist who owned several pharmacies, that made millions of dollars, approached me. He wanted to work with me. In exchange, he agreed to show me the secret sauce. I took his card and slept on it. But I also remembered that wasn't what I wanted anymore. My calling was to show people a more holistic and natural approach to living and healing. I never called.

A few months later, a friend called out of the blue and asked if I would be interested in working in Japan. It seemed so random. I didn't take it seriously, but told him I wouldn't mind learning more about the opportunity. Later that day, I received an email from him to set up a phone interview with the hospital in Japan.

After they finished telling me about the job and benefits, I asked, "Where specifically are you located in Japan?

He answered, "Okinawa."

I had just read a book about a community of people in Okinawa that had the largest group of centenarians (people who live to 100) in the world. And what was interesting about them, in particular, is they ate primarily a plant-based diet.

He only had a small fraction of my attention up to that point; but now, I was fully engaged and interested. I told him to give me some time to think about it, but he reached out consistently for over four months. Every time I had a rebuttal as to why I couldn't go, he gave me a solution. In an effort to run him off, I finally gave him what I believed to be an astronomical salary figure. When I told him the number, his reply was, "How soon could you be here?"

I was all out of excuses. It honestly started to feel like this was everything I asked for. After all, I'd said I wanted to work abroad. They agreed to me only working 14 days a month so

I could have a two-week vacation every month. And the icing on the cake was I would have the opportunity to study the nutritional habits of people who actually lived a plant-based lifestyle and reaped the benefits.

I made the decision to take the job. However, when I began telling my friends, my university, and others, they frowned at the idea. They believed it was a foolish mistake. Especially after receiving an award and getting invited to be a part of some special inner professional circles. Everyone believed I was being immature and throwing my career down the drain. I even had someone tell me I was being selfish and self-centered.

It became stressful thinking about having to potentially say no to what seemed to be the dream I manifested into reality. I even made up justifications like "it's too good to be true."

I took a getaway to clear myself from all the clutter. Once I was alone, all the fog lifted and clarity set in. My heart, mind, and spirit were saying leave and go with a clear conscience. Less than two months later I sold everything, my house, car, and jumped on the plane. Even though I knew it was the right decision, it still felt like I let everyone down.

GOING BEYOND FEAR & LEARNING TO FLY

I arrived in Okinawa with four large suitcases and a lot of uncertainty about leaving behind a very promising career.

Quitting my job raised so many fears: homelessness, unworthiness, instability, insecurity, poor decision-making, and the list goes on. It felt like I was drowning in quicksand. The whole time I reminded myself that this is what starting over and creating a new beginning feels like. It's uncomfortable, confusing, and stressful. That was primarily because of my unwillingness to let one door close so another could open.

The first few months, I barely left the house. I felt guilty any time I enjoyed myself. One day while watching the sunset on my balcony, I told myself to let go of the need to have everyone else's approval. Life is not a rehearsal or photoshoot. You only get one shot.

Since I practiced karate growing up and knew that Okinawa was known historically for being influential in the evolution of karate with mythic figures like Mr. Miyagi from the movie *The Karate Kid*, I joined a local dojo and learn from a karate master.

When I arrived for my first lesson, the sensei asked me in Japanese to leave my shoes and mind at the door. Confused, I spent most of that practice trying to figure out how to leave my mind at the front door.

Ironically, I felt like him asking me to do it only helped to make me bring more of my mind into practice. Later I asked one of the other students, "Why does sensei ask us to leave our shoes and minds at the door?"

He told me with a straight face, "Because you might have shit on them."

I laughed but the simplicity of the statement made it all click.

In life, there are environments or rooms we want to be in, but most of us aren't willing to pay the cost to go into them. We say we want to be healed but aren't willing to let go of the things that cause the imbalance in the first place.

The lesson was obvious. To be a student at the dojo, we had to leave our shit at the door. Everything we thought we knew about karate, our fears, egos, doubts, and anything else that might interfere with receiving guidance and developing as a student had to be surrendered.

This is how every area of life works. If you want peace, you must be willing to remove your attachment to drama, disharmony, and being the victim. This doesn't mean that you weren't the victim of a crime, it simply means you don't have to attach yourself to the identity of being a victim. When you say you want to live in the room of love, you have to check your hate at the door because the two extremes cannot coexist.

Letting go, allowing, and finding alignment with the higher version of myself is how I was able to get what I truly wanted out of life. I had spent my entire life asking, "why me," and in one moment I received an epiphany about it all.

It happened one day when I was on the beach while living in Okinawa. Staring out into the ocean, I had a flash of every major life event I had gone through. I was able to see every experience with a new understanding and its purpose attached to it. It felt like all the answers I had forgotten while taking an important test flooded into my brain all at once. The entire moment felt surreal. After all, I was the kid from the projects who got out the hood, became a doctor, traveled the world, and was now living on the beach in Japan.

On that day, it was just me, water, and a liberated mind. No shaman, guru, or spiritual teacher. Just me with God whispering into my consciousness. I came into the greatest knowing of them all: "YOU ARE ENOUGH and everything that happened was for YOU."

We've all heard this before. Knowing this, not just thinking it, removes all the self-inflicted roadblocks we put in place to sabotage our own growth. It helps us believe in our own self-sustainability to endure tough times and understand failure as a necessary function of success. It also reveals the parts of ourselves we've disowned that block us from getting to know who we truly are. I think it's amazing that we all seem to walk down different roads to discover the same truths.

From that moment on, I've had some of the best moments of my life.

While in Japan, I traveled to over 40 countries. I made friends all around the world. Studied herbal medicine and holistic healing with some of the world's best natural doctors and did things I could only dream of. However, I almost voluntarily canceled my own dreams to make other people happy and me sad in the process.

I learned earlier in life the importance of not allowing other's opinions of me to influence what I believed I deserved. Now I was learning not to allow other's opinions of me to influence the *choices* I made.

FALL DOWN 8 TIMES, GET UP 9

One of our deepest fears is the fear of failure. Not because we believe it's capable of doing any physical damage, but because of the potential psychological pain we believe it causes when we're judged by others and ourselves for not succeeding. So instead of taking a leap, we sell ourselves short on any occasion we can. We avoid the challenges presented to us in life and go for the sure thing. We mask our fears in practicality by blaming our kids, applying for safe jobs we know we'll hate, and then reminding everyone else it was the smart thing to do.

We then project our fears on anyone who would dare to go after their hopes and dreams and make us feel inadequate for not going after ours. It's not always our enemies that show up as opposition. Parents do this to children, husbands do this to wives, and vice versa. And it's not because they don't love you or don't have your best interest at heart. In their minds, they believe this is an act of love and they're protecting you. The truth is, it doesn't matter if it comes from an external force or if it's self-inflicted. The fear of failure paralyzes our potential for growth and blinds us to our own greatness.

There's an acronym I love for the word F.E.A.R. which is "False Evidence Appearing Real." This acronym speaks to the tangled web of illusions our minds create before anything in reality has actually happened. Most of our fears aren't based on anything that has actually happened to us in the past or the present. Most of our fears are based on what our minds believe will happen in the future. That is the quintessential definition of an illusion. Although the fear is completely imaginary, the psychological effects are very real. There is a psychology behind our fear of failure that is deeply rooted in our own self-worth.

It's not the actual act of failing that incites fear in us. It's how we feel as a result of failing that strikes fear into our psyche. The fear of failure is really the fear of feeling shame and unworthiness. These emotions are often triggered as a result of not succeeding.

I grew up in an era where whoopings were not only legal but celebrated by other parents. I was as mischievous as they come; so, I had my fair share. What I remember most is that the physical beating didn't hurt nearly as much as the disappointment I felt from my parents. It was the shame of not being the child they wanted me to be that cut the deepest. Shame is a toxic emotion because instead of feeling regret about what you did, you feel bad about YOU.

What I want to teach you in this chapter is that you don't have to go 82-0 to be a champion. There's a huge difference between falling and failing. I don't like the connotation behind the word *fail*. It implies that the act is complete and as a result, either my effort was or I am now a failure.

On the other hand, falling is a natural occurrence. We see it as a minor hiccup along our journey. When a toddler learns to walk, we don't throw the whole baby away when it stumbles and falls for the first time. We know learning to walk is a process and we accept the falls as necessary lessons. This is why we should embrace the idea of falling in every aspect of our lives. It's often said that success leaves clues. If that's the case, then our falls are the breadcrumbs along that path. A fall doesn't tell us we failed. It shows us we pushed beyond the boundaries of our comfort zones to explore new possibilities.

Instead of shaming ourselves for striving, we should master the art of falling forward closer towards success. In martial arts, students are taught how to fall without injuring themselves and in certain situations are encouraged to fall. This practice is called ukemi—the art of falling. I learned in karate that knowing how to fall was just as important as knowing how to stay upright. You're also taught the safest and most effective way to get back up. These same principles can be applied to life because falling is part of life and sometimes it can be used to our advantage.

It's important to first understand the lesson in why we fall and second that we should always get our asses back up. World-renowned motivational speaker Les Brown would say, "If you can look up, you can get up!"

Falling isn't a sign of weakness, incompetence, or a shortage of self-worth. Not getting up can be. Push through and pop up as soon as you hit the ground. Don't allow shame or self-pity to settle in. You're a warrior. Get up. Brush yourself off. Put your hands up, tuck your chin and let the challenges of life know they're wasting their time getting in your way.

Be prepared to hit the canvas again if need be. Just make sure you go down swinging because what you truly want in life will require the kind of effort most people aren't willing to give. So instead of avoiding the inevitable, I want you to be prepared mentally for anything. Sure enough, one day someone or something is going to try to break you.

Every origin story from Superman to Black Panther has that pivotal moment where they can choose to be broken or lean into the bend. Warriors bend but never break. Falling builds character and strength to stand tall. This is why we root for characters like Sylvester Stallone in movies like *Rocky*. We want him to get up every time he's knocked down because we see ourselves in him as the underdog. Like him, we know what it's like to be knocked down and counted out. We don't celebrate Rocky's wins. We celebrate him getting up. In one *Rocky* scene, he wins a fight simply because he got up and his opponent didn't.

They made six sequels to the movie *Rocky*. Nine, if you count the spin-off sequels of Creed. I've seen all of those movies at least once. I love watching the underdog fall and always get up because it reminds me of my own life. There's been eight times in my life where I took a fall. Each time I honestly didn't know if I would get back up.

- The first time was when I was arrested at 11-years-old.

- The second time I fell was when I saw my friend, Corey, kill another friend of mine in the seventh grade.

- The third time I fell was when my cousin, Donald, was killed in a car chase with the police.

- I fell for a fourth time a few months later when I was placed in the educatable retarded class.

I praise the younger version of myself for standing up and realizing that despite the hurt and feeling of unworthiness I was experiencing, there was still a lot left in me. Where the courage and conviction came from, I don't know. But, that day changed the trajectory of my life. Being told you're not smart is one thing. Being placed in that class for me felt like a nail in the coffin. They were trying to bury me while I was still alive. Although I felt dead inside.

The experience taught me that someone else's opinion of you is like a butt hole. Everybody's got one. The only opinion that matters is yours. People don't know what you've been through, conquered, or the seeds that have been planted in you, or the purpose God has in store for you.

- The fifth time I fell was when I broke my neck fighting. Take home message: unlearning is just as important as learning.

- The sixth time I fell was when I became homeless. It's okay not to be okay. I had to learn the hard way, but I learned.

- The seventh time I fell was after going from homeless to homeowner. I had to sell my homes when the real estate bubble popped.

Did you know that seven is the number of completion, both physically and spiritually? I wished I had known this when I was going through this fall. It would've given me more clarity on why I needed to go through this experience. Especially after going through a brief period of homelessness. This was a huge lesson in trust and allowing the goodness of life to work its magic.

- The eighth time I fell was when I didn't go with the flow and quit my promising career after becoming a pharmacist.

At the time it felt like I was spiraling out of control, plummeting into a permanent failure. The number eight signifies the start of new beginnings. And that's exactly what it was. The eighth time I fell started a whole new era in my life.

In Japan there is a proverb called "Nana korobi ya oki." The literal translation is "fall down seven times, get up eight." It embodies the concept of resilience and insistence that no matter how many times you get knocked down, you must get up again.

I've been knocked down so much in life, I honestly stopped counting. The eight times I shared with you are the times I didn't think I would get back up. It doesn't matter if you think you'll get back up or not. The only thing that matters is that you always do.

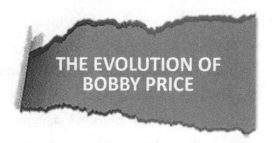

THE EVOLUTION OF BOBBY PRICE

When I left my job in Okinawa, I decided to travel the world and learn everything I could from herbalists, holistic healers, village medicine men, shamans, and gurus. At every opportunity, I was speaking to anyone who would listen about using food as medicine.

I went to China to learn about Traditional Chinese Medicine, Indonesia for Balinese Traditional Healing, Thailand for understanding how to incorporate herbs in food, India for yoga and meditation, and several countries in Africa to learn herbal medicine.

The entire time I thought my journey was just about learning how to heal others, I was healing myself in the process. Emotional traumas, mental barriers, and mental ailments evaporated almost without me noticing. I finally felt like who I always knew I was: peaceful, connected, and tapped into a higher source.

It was finally time to go back to America to share all the ancient wisdom that had completely shifted my life. Yet, everything in me was resistant to the idea. Between the numerous murders of unarmed African-Americans by police and the election of President 45, the environment in America was far more toxic than I believed I could bear. It had been almost five years since I lived in America and the time was already reminding me of how dangerous it is to simply be black.

Another epiphany. Whenever your calling comes, a barrier or mental justification will arise to stop you in your tracks. We must remind ourselves the term is calling because we have to answer. In order for you to break through and get shift going in your life, you have to be unstoppable when it comes to serving your purpose. This doesn't mean you have to run through a brick wall or swim through the fiery pits of hell. It just means never stop in the pursuit of your calling.

I booked the ticket and a few weeks later, boarded my 16-hour flight back to the U.S. I couldn't sleep during the flight. I spent the whole time thinking about how to share my gift with the world. I knew almost instantly it had to be a book. There's only one of me but I could share my story and lessons with millions without ever having to leave my home.

There was a huge problem. I wasn't an author and didn't even do well in my English courses in college. I had been gone for almost five years. Would people even remember me? Who was going to buy a book about using food as medicine and eliminating animal-based products from their diet? I could barely get people I knew to listen to me before I moved away. How was I going to get a stranger to not only listen but adopt the principles I was teaching?

To be honest, outside of myself I wasn't very successful with my message up to this point. As a matter of fact, the very first event I planned in 2012 was an epic failure. At the beginning of my health journey, I helped a few people here and there. One of them was gracious enough to offer me a meeting space to have an event. The room was huge! It had a capacity for roughly 300 people, give or take. I passed out thousands of flyers and spoke to hundreds of people. Then on the day of the event, only four people showed up.

For a very brief moment, I was shattered. I changed my perspective. Four people actually showed up! I went on with the presentation as if the room was filled to capacity. All four of the attendees thanked me and asked tons of questions afterward. That experience taught me to show up for those who show up for me.

Don't worry about how many people follow you or how many likes you get. Just focus on being true to yourself as an instrument of transformation and inspiration for others.

With that in mind, I decided it didn't matter if four or 4,000 people bought my book. I would consider it a success even if I only changed one life. Once I touched down on U.S. soil, I put all my energy and resources into finishing my book. I knew if I wanted to complete the book in the time I set for myself, getting a job would not be an option. I didn't want any distractions to stop me from answering my calling.

I was fortunate that I had been saving my entire time in Japan. But after traveling the world for over a year, my cash reserves had dwindled below my comfort level. I gave myself a monthly budget.

You know, life always happens; car troubles here and a torn Achilles there were thrown into the mix. I had also grossly underestimated what it costs to write a book. Ultimately, my monthly budget went out the window. I overpaid people who did their job horribly and ended up having to pay for someone else to redeem the work they didn't do. I made several mistakes throughout the process. Instead of taking them as losses, I took them all as lessons. I learned so many ways of how not to write a book. It ultimately helped me create my own process for how to write a book in 30 days.

Once I had the final draft, I sent it to the editor for review. In the meantime, I went into strategy mode to figure out how to make this book successful. As part of my book launch, I decided to do a book cover contest with the small audience I had at the time. My graphic designer created three options to choose from and ultimately, I selected the one my audience chose. This played a double role by helping me understand which book cover the average person would be most attracted to (people do judge a book by its cover) and it also created awareness that a book was coming.

Next, I opted to do a book signing event. Most book signings happen in conjunction with a bookstore. Attendees usually show up, purchase a book from the bookstore, get a reading from the author, and ask a few questions. That wouldn't be enough for what I was doing. I was facing a massive uphill battle trying to convince people, especially in the African-American community, to show up for a book signing on not eating meat. I witnessed the struggle firsthand for years. Soul food is just as much a part of our culture as dancing, music, and ingenuity.

This was going to have to be an event. Almost like a town hall meeting with a huge call-to-action. I wanted attendees to know it wasn't just guns and drugs that were killing us. Diabetes, high blood pressure, and cancer were even bigger enemies because they're often silent but deadly. And typically, we put all the blame on our family genes without looking into the true causes.

Having the event would be a great opportunity for me to explain how the book titled *Vegucation Over Medication* was a roadmap back to health using the same natural approach our ancestors historically used since the beginning of time.

One month out from the event, I got the final edits from the editor. In the first five pages, I found 37 proofreading or grammatical errors. I was pissed. I returned the document back to the editor. When I got it back, to be honest, it wasn't much better.

For a moment, I went into panic mode. We had already sold a few tickets to the book signing and I like to keep my promises. There wasn't enough time to vet another editor. So, I reached out to five of my closest friends who loved to read and we scoured through the draft like a forensics team.

I reminded myself "progress, not perfection" is the goal. That's tough to tell a Virgo but I went with it anyway. The message was far more important than my personal need for perfection. I'm so thankful for my inner circle. I think friends are God's way of compensating for our family.

Getting to a final draft I was comfortable with and a winning book cover, it was time to get physical copies of the book printed. I was told it typically takes 2-3 weeks to get your first copies. It was perfect timing. I'd just made the deadline. I ordered 222 copies. Don't ask me why. It just seemed like a great number. Plus, I was now scraping the bottom of my bank account; I needed this to work.

Seven days out from the event and I still had no books. I reached out to the printing company and was told there was an unforeseeable delay. The books wouldn't arrive until three or four days after the book signing. To make things worse, we had only sold 23 tickets. I was out of options. All the negative emotions associated with panic creeped in and destroyed my positivity. I put my team on notice that I was thinking about canceling the event and returning everyone's money.

I slept on it before deciding and hoped the universe would conspire to rearrange reality in such a way that the event would be possible. In the middle of the night between three and four a.m., I woke up and heard what seemed like a whisper, "Find a local printer." I went straight to Google and found three options. The first two told me it would take 7-10 days and each book would be almost double the cost I spent with the initial printing company. When I called the third company, a man answered and told me to come into his office to tell him about my book. It was an interesting request from a printer.

Once I met with him and shared my story, he said he would make sure my books were printed by the day before my event for the same cost I paid initially. The only challenge I had now was where the hell was I going to get the money to pay him? I had already paid money for plant-based food options to be prepared by an amazing chef for the event. I had paid for the event space in full, a photographer, videographer, along with a list of other items that had wiped out my funds.

My best friend, Ponle, came to my aid. He had watched me write for countless hours, make sacrifices, and pour myself into this project. He was just as much a part of it as I was. So, with one swipe, everything was in place.

Remember, that help always appears while you're working, not worrying. It always inspires people to watch someone's relentless pursuit of their purpose.

After that, everything fell into alignment. Every day, more and more tickets were sold and 24 hours before the book signing, the event sold out. When I walked into the event space, attendees were shoulder-to-shoulder. Everyone was smiling, engaged in conversation, and there was a buzz of heightened energy that made the hairs on the back of my neck stand up.

There were baby boomers, millennials, and everyone in between. By the end of the event, I sold every book and product I had. The entire room erupted with applause when I finished my presentation. I couldn't believe it. In the moment, it felt so surreal. I wondered if I was going to snap out of it and wake up. Everything happened exactly as I imagined it. The impact could easily be measured by the level of excitement and number of questions the audience asked as I signed books and took pictures.

I made more money in one day than I had ever made in a month, although I never focused on the money. My motto was when you focus on the outcome, you never have to worry about income. That day was the epitome of the phrase.

A few days after the event, I was invited to speak in Switzerland at a medical conference. They offered to pay for all my travel and lodging expenses and pay me several thousand dollars to attend. When I asked how they discovered me, the lady told me they heard about me from a raw food restaurant owner in Cape Town, South Africa.

When I was in Cape Town studying herbal medicine with the "Sack People" on Table Top Mountain, I also took a raw foods class at a local restaurant. During the class, I wanted to share everything I knew about using food as medicine. At times, I must've taken over the class unknowingly. I was the last person to leave and continued the conversation with the owner, Roxy. She never forgot me and ended up telling her friends in Switzerland about me. How amazing is that?

Here's the icing on the cake. The date I was to speak just so happened to be on my birthday. Reality is sometimes even more unbelievable than our imaginations.

Looking back, I now grasp how at times what I thought was insignificant or a setback was actually a setup for a come up. I was being prepared for a transformational life shift I didn't know was coming. Every life experience was simply preparing me for my ultimate destiny.

My Shift Years in Retrospect
Sifting for the Lessons

As you remove things that no longer serve you and prevent you from getting into the rooms you want to be in, you'll probably notice you have a pile of shit sitting at the door.

Leave it all behind. Make your peace with it. Ask yourself, "Who am I now without the pile of shit I left sitting at the door?"

Do you feel lighter? Can you imagine all the new possibilities you could experience now without the weight of the burdens you've been carrying?

This is what embracing life as your guru is all about. Taking your own life experiences, extracting the mountains of wisdom from them, and leaving behind anything that doesn't serve you.

Most of us never learn the lessons. If we do, it's after the experience has happened repeatedly (when life experiences repeat themselves, it's life, our guru, saying you didn't get the lesson). At that point, we often become so damaged by the experience, we learn the wrong lessons. Instead of learning patience or proper discernment, we think the take-home message is not to trust people. This is why it's so important for us to be mindful during all our experiences. That way we can see the lessons during the experience or even better before they happen.

I know how difficult it can be to practice mindfulness amid all of life's struggles. We all get lost in the sauce of what's happening and forget to learn the lessons. But when we position ourselves as conscious observers of life instead of being reactionary participants, we'll always see the moral of the story in every part of our journey.

The best example of this is like buying tickets to go see a Broadway play like "Venus" by Suzan-Lori Parks or "A Raisin In The Sun" by Lorraine Hansberry. When you arrive at the theater, you know without a doubt you'll be sitting in the audience and the actors will be on the stage. Sometimes the performances are so compelling you feel like you're on the stage and everything is happening to you. I once saw Denzel Washington perform on Broadway in "Julius Caesar". His acting was so convincing when they called for an intermission, I had to snap out of it and realize it was a play.

Being a conscious observer of your own life experiences is like choosing to be in the audience of a play instead of being an actor on stage. The word actor comes from the Latin word "agere" or the Latin root "act" meaning to "act, do, or doer."

When you're doing instead of being, it's very difficult to be conscious of the experience. This is what makes us so reactionary and we end up saying and doing things we later regret. Instead of being an actor, pull yourself off stage and become a witness. Consciously observe each experience. Seek understanding first, instead of wanting to be understood, and the lesson will appear as vividly as the sun in a clear blue sky.

My first conscious experience with this philosophy happened at an airport in Bangkok, Thailand in 2015. I was on my way back to Okinawa after snorkeling in Phi Phi Island, visiting elephant sanctuaries, and bamboo rafting through the Phuket jungle.

When I arrived at the airport, it was absolute madness. The lines for every ticketing agent stretched throughout the airport with no signs of movement. I typically arrive at the airport three hours in advance, but the taxi driver had mistakenly taken me to Don Mueang Airport initially instead of Suvarnabhumi Airport.

Since I now only had two hours before departure, I jumped into the first line I saw and threw my headphones on. The lines moved at a snail's pace. People were getting antsy and frustrated with the possibility of missing their flights. As the pace for some lines picked up, you saw the lines merge in an attempt for passengers to get in lines that had begun to move. Periodically, the person in front of me turned around to voice his frustrations to me, but I couldn't hear a damn thing he said with my headphones on. Yet, I still nodded here and there in agreement.

Suddenly, our line started moving so quickly everybody in front of me unwrinkled their faces and were smiling. Abruptly, a man standing to the left of me walked in front of me and said, "You broke me and my family in line."

I told him he was mistaken. The person in front of me also confirmed that I had been behind him the entire time. He pretended like he didn't hear either of us.

I won't go into detail about what I said to him next, but it was enough for him to grab his family and run to the airport attendant. The attendant came to ask me what happened, and the person in front of me explained that the man was lying. In response, the attendant took the man closer to the front of the next line. For some reason, that pissed me off. Watching him get rewarded for being deceitful seemed unfair. Oddly enough, despite him being pushed to the front, I ended up checking in before he did. I made sure I gave him a little smirk once I was handed my ticket.

While going through security, the whole incident kept replaying in my mind. I no longer felt good about what happened. It felt like it was a test and I failed. I asked myself, "How would the highest version of myself have handled the situation?" Even better, "What would he do about it now?"

I wished for another opportunity to be better, even though I felt like the guy was also at his worst. We can't control what others do, but we can always control how we respond. Responding with awareness for the purposes of keeping my peace and not being distracted by bullshit is always the goal. I told myself I'd make this right moving forward.

When I boarded the plane, I felt a little lighter knowing I had made a new commitment to myself. As I approached my seat, 10D, guess who happened to be seated right next tome? You guessed right, the asshole from earlier.

Life definitely has a sense of humor, I thought. And like many other times in life, I was being given another opportunity to learn the lesson intended for me to learn from the beginning. This is what I mean when I say, if you don't learn the lesson sent to expand you the first time, the experience will continue to repeat itself. With each repeat, the experience gets more abrasive and costly. I was so shocked at the irony. This was my guru (life) saying, "Put your money where your mouth is." So, I did.

I told him, "I wish I'd handled the situation differently. I don't want you to be afraid of me or feel uncomfortable during the flight. We should've been better examples, at least for your kids."

"I apologize for lying. I just wanted to get my family home," he replied.

"I overstand, enjoy your flight," I replied.

Once we settled our differences, I gave him my aisle seat so he could sit closer to his family. It immediately felt like the karmic balance of the entire universe was re-established. I felt better energetically and learned a very valuable lesson about the language life chooses to speak to us.

Afterwards, I thought about how many beefs could've been squashed using this train of thought. How many relationships could've been saved, altercations avoided, misunderstandings corrected, and stress relieved.

What about you? How many hardships could've been avoided if you took this same approach?

The wisdom we receive when we open our eyes to the lessons right in front of us is like getting a divine download straight from God. First, we have to be willing students of life in order to receive them.

Part II

My Life is a Guru Philosophy

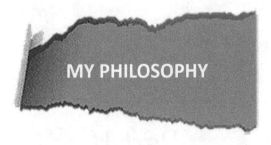

MY PHILOSOPHY

What if I told you life has a language that's spoken and embedded within each experience we're taken through on our respective journeys? The nature of these experiences is to teach us the lessons we need to know to rise above our individual and collective traumas and to evolve. The more we listen and pay attention to the lessons life wants us to learn, the less painful the lessons become. We also won't have to continue repeating experiences in greater severity to get the same lessons before they're learned.

Life is the teacher, mentor, sensei, and guru we never asked for but always needed. It speaks in a language that is easy to decode, but still difficult for us to translate. We spend most of our lives attached to our negative experiences constantly asking ourselves, "Why did this experience happen to me?" But we rarely ask why good happens. We readily accept any good experiences as if they're gifts we're entitled to. However, we view our struggles and challenges as forms of divine punishment or simply bad luck. As soon as something bad happens, we drop down to our knees praying to God, asking for new circumstances and immediate change. We never think to ask ourselves, "Could this unpleasant experience be a part of our personal and spiritual development?"

I believe we're all spiritual beings having a human experience. Not human beings having a spiritual experience. This changes absolutely everything. From this standpoint, we view our essence as an infinite soul instead of just a body. The soul is not bound by a body. It's multi-sensory with a higher level of consciousness, directly connected to Source. The body is bound by laws of nature, susceptible to getting sick, limited by five senses, and every day a step closer to the grave. The soul comes into human form to experience limitation. Our limitation is experienced as pain, struggle, challenges, happiness, love, doubt, joy, etc.

Most people believe they have a soul; but, most people also think the soul is in the body, dormant until they die. I believe before we start our human journey, our soul decides whether we'll be black or white, tall or short, American or Asian, and even who our parents will be.

I also believe we make agreements with other souls to be a part of our tribe during our human experience. Our tribe members agree to take part in certain experiences and relationships before they ever happen. All of this is done with the intent to create a divine curriculum that advances and develops the individual soul and collective as a whole.

This reinforces the idea that everything and everyone is connected, and everything happens for a reason. Life isn't this chaotic, random string of events that we once thought it was. Our life experiences are essentially the curriculum that life, as a guru, uses to evolve us as students. As a student, whenever we have lessons that continually repeat themselves, like bad relationships or being cut off in traffic every morning, this is our guru saying, "You aren't learning the lessons I'm trying to teach you." Patience, acceptance, letting go, allowing forgiveness, vulnerability, and expansion are often the lessons life is trying to teach us.

We become who we are not based solely on our experiences, but more so on how we respond to them. For example, you could easily have two kids from the same neighborhood, similar parental structures, identical socioeconomic status, comparable traumas, matching IQs, and resembling triumphs. Yet, their paths in life will be totally different because of their differences in perceptions and responses to their experiences.

We base how we perceive and respond to our life experiences according to the mindset we have when we approach those experiences. Of course, our circumstances will have an impact; ultimately, our mindset determines how we respond. Remember, it's always about how you respond, not what happened. That is the major key.

Why? Because our greatest barrier in life will always be the limitations we place upon ourselves based on our past experiences. We can't go backwards into the past to change what happened. Nor forward to the future to alter it. We can't switch out our parents for better ones or the drug-infested neighborhoods we grew up in for the suburbs. What we all have is the ability to change our mindsets no matter what we've gone through.

Choosing to approach life with the mindset that life is my guru allows you to receive wisdom from your life experiences and become a higher version of yourself through that knowledge instead of becoming attached to the struggles of your experiences.

What's on the other side of receiving wisdom that comes with this approach? The version of yourself you've always dreamed of. The mood and energy you've always wanted. Healing and a tremendous amount of peace to replace the bound negativity of past traumas and dramas. All that is required is for you to let go and embrace the wisdom of the guru (life). The most difficult part is often letting go because we're so addicted to being attached. Even when it is to our detriment. Sharing my story in Part I was me illustrating what letting go could look and feel like.

YOU ARE WHAT YOU EAT

We've all heard sayings like "you are what you eat" and "food is medicine." These are ancient philosophies passed down by our ancestors to impart wisdom on the significant impact our food choices have on our overall well-being. In my first book, *Vegucation Over Medication*, I offer in-depth knowledge of why eating plant-based is the best way to achieve healing in your body and is the gateway to totally transforming your life.

Food is defined as a nourishing substance consumed by animals or absorbed by plants for sustaining life and growth. That definition differs greatly from how most people think about food. For most people, food is a source of entertainment to cure boredom, the centerpiece for social gatherings and celebrations, an opportunity to quench the pleasures of our tastebuds, a way of identifying one's culture and family tradition, or a method of self-soothing during emotional hardships.

Food is much more than that. Food is the other partner in the most intimate relationship we'll ever have. We put food inside of our bodies and it literally becomes the blood that courses through our veins, the tissues and bones that make up our structure, and the organ systems that give us life.

Even more than that, food is information. It tells our bodies about both our internal and external environments. It can trigger our DNA to turn cancer genes on or off like a light switch. The foods we choose can also determine our mood. Ninety percent of the "happy molecule" Serotonin that helps to keep a smile on your face is made in the gut using the nutrients you consume, along with the good bacteria in your gut's lining.

The bottom line here is if you eat living foods, they give you life. However, you are what you eat isn't just about food. It's about being a relentless gatekeeper for what you allow in your temple (body). What you eat, listen to, and watch are all forms of food. The quality of your choices will determine if your food is the highest form of healing or the slowest method of poisoning. How it enters the body doesn't matter, whether it's through your mouth, ears, or eyes. What you consume will become you. And whatever is inside of you will be revealed to the world.

We reveal ourselves in every choice we make. Especially those that contribute to our thoughts, beliefs, and health. Making a healthy food choice is an act of self-love. So, it's not just an orange. It is the content of the orange that either provides nourishment or DIS-EASE within you. Think about it from this perspective, if you squeeze an orange, you'll always get orange juice. The same goes for an apple. We all know the content of an apple, so we know what to expect.

The question is when life squeezes you, and it will, what will come out of you?

If you were to squeeze me earlier in my life, I'm not sure what would've oozed out of me: sadness and heartbreak, and maybe even a little chicken gravy. Unlike an apple or orange, we can actually change what's inside of us. I wish I had known this 20 years ago. Like many, I never took the time to unpack my emotions. I pretended everything was okay when it wasn't, even when someone asked me if I was okay.

I used the same coping mechanisms everyone else around me used. I never thought for a moment that adopting an unhealthy habit from friends and family could potentially become generational curses. We can't ever change the choices we've made in the past or the things that happened to us, but we can take ownership of our own redemption and rewrite our stories moving forward.

THE POWER OF OUR EVERYDAY CONSUMPTION

Once I adopted new standards for what I would accept in my temple as it relates to food, many of the same criteria I used for choosing breakfast, lunch, and dinner also applied to every aspect of my life. My selection of music changed. I didn't want to listen to gangster rap anymore. It had become too violent for this version of me. Instead, I listened to music that was peaceful, fun, harmonious, and had a message consistent with growth and love. Conscious hip-hop, neo soul, jazz, and binaural beats became my selections. I changed the podcasts I listened to and even the conversations I was willing to have. I wanted positivity so I spoke positivity. Not only into my life but into the lives of anyone I came into contact with, even strangers.

Every day, we make food choices that either make health deposits or health withdrawals. Again, when I say food choices, I don't just mean the food we consume. It's also the things we feed ourselves through our eyes: television, movies, and social media. The ideas and thoughts we feed ourselves through thinking, reading, music, and conversation. The words we choose to speak into existence bounce back with the same energy as does the food we eat.

We never think of television, commercials, or movies as pro-gramming, but they are. And we never ask ourselves what these programs are asking us to do. This is why you must become a ruthless gatekeeper of anything that comes into your temple. You have to view your body as a temple in order to do that. It's not a garbage can. These are just some of the new thoughts that were downloading whenever I meditated or prayed.

Along with my changes in food and music, I even had the urge to practice yoga…which I fought tooth and nail for a while. The urge was my body's way of seeking a more restorative form of exercise opposed to my usual weightlifting and basketball regimen.

My inner dialogue also shifted dramatically. I believe we all have a minimum of two voices (or conversations) going on in our heads. One is feeding us fear, negativity, doubt, and scarcity. The other is feeding us faith, love, balance, and abundance. Faith and fear are two different types of beliefs.

Faith is simply the belief in the outcome our hearts' desire. Whereas, fear is the illusion we create and the belief in the outcome we don't desire. You know what else changed? My relationships. They didn't change because I was judgmental about the choices others were making. They changed because I realized a lot of my friendships were toxic, having been built on attachment, not genuine connection.

My priorities and goals also changed. They shifted towards things that were not only good for me, but good for everyone. I prioritized my well-being over money, acceptance, and societal approval. Most importantly, this all changed how I felt about myself.

We live in a society and culture designed to make us feel like we're not enough unless we buy or obtain things outside of ourselves. I spent my whole life thinking that if I got three or four degrees, became a doctor, wore a white coat, and made six figures, I could wash off the stench of being a project kid. Now, I realize I didn't need any of that bullshit. But obtaining those goals helped me see I could do anything, so they were a necessary part of my journey. I've always been a good soul and I always will be. That feels good. So good you can almost touch it.

All my life, I thought living was about accumulating things and getting a dream job. Ironically, I can't ever remember dreaming about working. I do, however, remember a few nightmares. My dreams were about the things I'm passionate about (healing) and the seeds of purpose that were planted into my heart. I wanted to become the Indiana Jones of natural medicine by traveling the world, discovering natural cures, and having wild adventures. And one year after changing what I ate and how I thought, I was moving to Japan to start that journey.

I'm not saying if you drink green smoothies and eat your veggies, you'll become some kind of superhero. What I know is that the phrase "You are what you eat" rings true for everyone. So, if what you eat is processed, fast, and cheap, then that's what you become. If you choose to eat salty, sugary, fatty foods that clog you, then you'll feel stagnant, blocked, and stuck. If you eat dead foods that lack vitality, then you'll suffer a slow death as hours, days, months, and years will be taken away from you by nutritional diseases.

If you listen to songs about heartbreak and violence, you'll be more prone to bitterness and anger. People who watch the news these days live in fear because much of what the news reports is based in fear-mongering. If you choose words that create doubt and promote negativity, you will struggle with procrastination and self-esteem issues.

However, if you eat living foods, they give you life. If you use your voice to uplift others and encourage yourself, you will feel capable and persevere through most of life's challenges.

If you listen to music that is about love, freedom, and having a good time, love will be drawn to you and your life will be joyful.

Being accountable for what you allow into your sacred space is the key to manifesting change. We can do this by aligning our thoughts, actions, and beliefs with the laws of attraction. Everything we project into the universe is what the universe sends back to us two-fold.

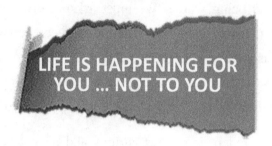

LIFE IS HAPPENING FOR YOU ... NOT TO YOU

One of the most powerful epiphanies I've ever had was coming into the knowing that, life isn't happening to you; it's happening for you.

This belief is so powerful because it made me realize in my lowest moments in life, I would instantly victimize myself in situations that caused me heartbreak, failure, or disappointment. It seems I believed being a victim was the only choice I had. This new perspective made me realize that each time I decided to default myself into victimhood, I took away my own power. I began noticing that I wasn't the only one doing this.

With this new understanding instead of asking, "Why does this always have to happen to me?" I now ask myself, "WHY NOT ME?"

If life isn't happening to me, it's happening for me. I'm now curious what lesson life is attempting to teach me with each new experience. Self-inquiry is a very important part of healing and being whole. We must ask ourselves the tough questions that we really don't want to know the answers to as curiosity is always what pushes and nudges us to evolve. And that's exactly what this new epiphany did for me. It pulled me out of victimhood and converted me into a student of life.

A great student is always curious and open to newfound wisdom. With this new shift in thinking, I saw a new perspective in all my life experiences. Especially unwanted experiences that were repeating. My perspective shifted from looking at those unwanted recurrences as punishment to hidden gifts in the form of lessons I was previously refusing to learn. So, they just kept on repeating themselves in hopes I would one day finally learn from those teachable moments.

Have you ever noticed when a life experience is continually repeating, the experience itself becomes more and more difficult? It's almost like the initial encounter is a gentle nudge that eventually turns into a backhanded slap. Since embracing this philosophy of life, I've learned that's how life teaches us. It doesn't want to punish us, but learning the lesson is a necessity. And many of us unfortunately don't learn until we suffer. So most times, we turn a gentle life experience into a UFC match gone bad because of our unwillingness to learn.

Embracing the idea that life is happening for me, and that all of my life experiences are a part of this masterful plan to help me grow and become the highest version of myself, changes the entire fabric of cause-and-effect in life. Nothing is insignificant; everything is part of the all-encompassing plan. It also means that God, whichever one you pray to or don't pray to, is conspiring on your behalf to create a path of least resistance towards more abundance.

What is even more fascinating about all of this, whether or not you believe it to be true, it has absolutely no impact on whether or not it is true. Some things in life are just universal law. What I know to be true is that when we change our minds, we always change our lives.

As Confucius said, "The man who believes he can, and the man who believes he can't, are both right." We are creators and capable of manifesting just about anything we can imagine. The only limitation we have is our own imagination. And we will always create in the direction of our thinking. This means if you say you want to be happy but you align all your thoughts and beliefs with sadness, then you'll be unhappy.

We'll dive more into how we properly align ourselves to create what we want instead of what we get by default in a later chapter. For now, I want you to think about some of the most challenging moments in your life. Ask yourself what it would be like if you looked at those tragedies from the perspective of 'this happened *for* me, not *to* me. It wasn't punishment. It was an experience of valuable wisdom.' Being on the other side of that experience now allows you to look back in hindsight with 20/20 vision and gain a tremendous amount of clarity around the importance of that experience for your own personal evolution.

I understand how traumatic it can be to dig up old experiences you thought you buried. Understand, if they are still triggering you emotionally, there's still healing left to do. When you feel the emotions start to boil, remain committed to healing. Stay open enough to receive wholeness and be brave enough to let it go. Remember, it happened *for* you, not *to* you. Letting go doesn't mean someone gets let off the hook, nor does it mean your feelings about what happened become invalid. Letting go just means the burden is too heavy to hold and still be able to move on. The only choice you have is to either hold on and stay stuck, or let go and be liberated.

None of what I'm recommending is easy. If it were, you would've already done it. The freedom that comes from letting go of our traumas and surrendering is priceless.

I wore my traumas like badges of honor. I was so proud of having survived them; I didn't want to let them go. They used to define who I was as a person so letting them go felt like I would lose myself in the process. However, the new thinking made me ask myself, "Who am I without my traumas?" It's like being from the worst area in the city, then going back years later to discover your entire neighborhood had been gentrified. For years you bragged about how dangerous it was, the people you knew, the wild experiences you had, and the nostalgic moments on corners during the heat of the summer. Now, all that has been replaced by coffee shops with expensive lattes and hipster, trust fund babies strolling up and down MLK Blvd. with their teacup yorkies.

I get why we all want to hold on to things that no longer serve us. Letting go and embracing a more nourishing point-of-view is the only pathway towards your redemption and discovering how beautiful you are without the wounds you carry. Erykah Badu paints a beautiful picture of this in her song "Bag Lady" where she describes metaphorically the emotional and spiritual dangers of carrying too much baggage. Checkout the lyrics (sing them if you can):

> *Bag lady you goin' hurt your back*
> *Draggin' all 'em bags like that*
> *I guess nobody ever told you*
> ***All you must hold on to***
> ***Is you, is you, is you.***
> *One day all 'em bag goin' get in your way*
> *One day all 'em bag goin' get in your way*

I said,

One day all 'em bag goin' get in your way

One day all 'em bag goin' get in your way

So

(Pack light, pack light)

Hmm, mmm

Bag lady, you goin' miss your bus

You can't hurry up

Cause you got too much stuff

I emphasized the line "All you must hold on to is you" because that is the greatest truth ever spoken.

Written on the walls of the temples of Ancient Egypt, "know thyself" is the golden rule of life. Knowing thyself isn't about knowing your personality, it's about knowing your heart. The part of you that is constant through this lifetime and beyond. We hold on to baggage because we don't know who we are without it. When we can't distinguish between ourselves and our life experiences, we think they're the same. But they're very different.

We're not the millions of experiences we go through. When we think we are, we end up like the Bag Lady. The bags get in our way and slow us down, causing us to almost miss our bus as Ms. Badu aka Fatbellybella says. We blame our high school teachers, our boss at work, all our ex-lovers, and we especially blame our parents.

Our parents often do the biggest number on us when it comes to emotional baggage. That's why our parents are our greatest teachers. They're often the source of our greatest traumas. None of us can change who our parents are. Attempting to reject your parents, valid or not, only creates more distance within yourself.

I say this realizing some of us got a really poor deal when it comes to our parents or whatever has happened to you. Let me be the first to say you are not the blame for your parents or most of the tragic experiences you've had to endure. Yet, we are always responsible for our own healing. That is not a job we can afford to lose or ever walk out on.

No one can heal for us. Not a therapist, an apology, or even money. We dance around actual healing by overcompensating with multiple college degrees, burying ourselves in our professional lives, buying material things, and even with our lovers.

Our unsuspecting lovers are usually the perfect tools for detaching ourselves from our need to heal. We throw away all the responsibility and tell them it's their job to make us happy, feel loved, achieve validation, and gain the sense of security that could only ever come from our own healing. We set them up to fail from the beginning. And when they inevitably do, we blame them for everything, including the things that happened before they even existed in our lives.

These are acts of self-sabotage that happen repeatedly. More accurately, these are lessons that repeat themselves continually until we embrace the wisdom that life is attempting to bless us with. We often get the same type of partners over and over because they reflect parts of ourselves we refuse to heal and lessons we chose to ignore.

We ignore these lessons because we believe that the experience is happening to us as punishment. However, if we could take just a moment and shift our thinking and energy towards embracing the wisdom from our experiences, we might learn something pretty profound, not just about ourselves, but about life itself.

Life is constantly speaking to us and teaching us in its own language. We tend to look at life through a black and white lens. We only see heads or tails, hot or cold, male and female, right or wrong, good or bad, and happy or sad. When quite often there's much more than meets the eye.

Life can create experiences for the sole purpose of testing our beliefs, not to see if we'll pass or fail, but to help us either reaffirm or decide to change a belief that isn't serving us.

To understand life speaks and teaches in its own language, we have to shift our thinking. That language is our experiences.

And quite often our most tragic experiences end up being our greatest teachers. How we perceive our struggles is what creates more struggle in life. Because the problem isn't the problem. How we perceive the problem is often the problem.

Do you think if you pray for love that God would respond by giving you love or by providing you with an opportunity to love? If you pray for more patience, do you think you'll be given patience or experiences that give you the opportunity to be patient?

STARTING

YOUR OWN

TRANSFORMATION

RISING ABOVE YOUR TRAUMAS

Contrary to popular belief. Most people prefer to be the victim opposed to the hero in their own life situations and stories. Being the victim comes with a few perks. You can defer all the blame and accountability, then pull a warm blanket of sympathy over your head until you completely disappear.

Being the victim gives you the perfect excuse to explain away your shortcomings of happiness, lack of great relationships and ability to stay committed, or the courage to take any leap beyond your comfort zone. It allows you to be special far beyond any other human being in existence because life is punishing you far more unfairly than anyone else.

This is why we ask ourselves as victims, "Why does this always happen to me?"

Being the victim creates stuckness in our decision-making process. If we create certain ways of thinking to deal with our childhood traumas and now, as adults, we're still using that same decision-making process, we're setting ourselves up to operate from victimhood and *stuckness*.

Going through a traumatic event like being molested, bullied, or abused by parents, affects us in ways we often don't comprehend. These types of traumas not only impact us growing up, they also impact our lives as adults.

What happened in the past doesn't always stay in the past. There are long term consequences for not addressing the effects of our traumatic experiences. Unresolved trauma comes out in different ways in relationships. Maybe you had a poor relationship with your mom. As a result, as a man, you may have a history of poor relationships with the women you've dated. You could also spend the rest of your life seeking approval and validation from women. These patterns of behavior create shame and guilt.

Unresolved trauma can also create narcissism. Instead of feeling shameful about ourselves, we end up thinking that the world ends and begins with us. It can also create a sense of grief. The life experiences we go through as children that we never get over or heal from create a psychological block that doesn't allow us to move on in life.

Putting yourself in a position of being a victim often makes you want to escape yourself. We often find routes to escape ourselves through food, relationships, or using illicit drugs.

Our past traumas and victimization can also affect our spirituality and our ability to connect with ourselves or others. It's very important to understand the need to address our traumas. When unaddressed, our traumas become the shadow parts of ourselves that we try to sweep under the rug. But they don't disappear. They end up ultimately causing us to destroy ourselves either consciously or unconsciously.

You may want to believe you're shielding yourself from certain areas out of a sense of protection. Essentially, what you do is put a band-aid over something that requires stitches.

We often settle for the option of treatment and end up falling short of healing. Treatment is not enough because it's like going out to get ice cream when you feel unhappy. Treatment only addresses the symptoms and ignores the actual cause. Which is why the trauma or dis-ease (lack of peace) persists indefinitely. Healing is actually dealing with the emotion, dealing with the grief, dealing with the hurt, and really dealing with what has broken you down. Healing requires us to have direct confrontation with the cause and shift ourselves back into alignment by changing our thoughts, behaviors, and beliefs. Healing helps you get back up. And the greatest barrier we have to any sort of healing comes out of the space of victimization.

Victimization is the resistance to healing. It's not us *not* wanting to be healed or *not* willing to do it. We're resistant to healing because we become so enamored with being a victim and getting sympathy and empathy from others. We get addicted to blaming others and creating excuses as to why we can't move on and grow in life.

A huge part of my healing process was becoming more intimate with my pain and my trauma. I spent most of my life trying to forget or avoid it, pretending like it didn't happen, and creating stories around it as well. The stories I created around my trauma centered me either as the victim or the hero in the situation. Most times, where I thought I was the person being hurt, I later recognized there were two people hurting in the situation.

From this recognition came a deeper understanding of the phrase hurt people hurt people. This understanding allowed me to lean into my pain. Leaning into my traumas allowed me to see exactly what they were. I had to peel back the layers, past the scars and scabs, to see how infected the original cuts were and if they had healed properly.

When we get cut and something sharp literally breaks through our skin, the body will send blood to the wounded location and then clotting will occur. Once the bleeding stops, the wound becomes a scab. At that point, the skin heals a little bit on its own, but it might require more to get it back to normal.

Many of us, in most cases, don't go through our healing processes completely. We want to believe we've healed because we saw the wound become the scab which to us represents progress. We don't allow the scab to become a scar. But scars not only represent lessons learned but physical and emotional damage that was done.

We also don't allow the wound to heal because we poke and itch at our wounds so much. We end up pulling off the scab because we don't trust the healing process. Experiencing the pain, grief, and any other emotion associated with the experience are all part of the process and can't be avoided.

We should all ask ourselves, "What did my traumatic experiences do to me?"

That's exactly what I had to decide to do in my life before I could see any real transformation. Instead of making all the traumatic and dramatic events of my life the reasons I didn't succeed, or glorifying them, (because we often glorify our traumas as badges of survivorship) I decided to look at them from a holistic perspective.

I didn't just look at them from my perspective. Because if you look at any traumatic situation from just your perspective, you get a very limited view. Imagine seeing a four-sided building on fire. On one side of the building there's an older lady. On another side there's a small child. The third side has a cat and on the fourth side there's a family. All of them need to be rescued.

When we only look at our traumas and experiences from one perspective (our own), we end up only addressing the symptoms without ever getting to the actual root cause.

Only looking at the building from the initial view (your perspective) means the other people in need of help are left unattended because you can only view two sides at most. Don't get me wrong, our perspectives are very valid. Although, if we look at our traumas a little deeper (from all perspectives), we'll find that we're able to save the entire building.

We're able to save everybody in the situation. To do that, we have to choose to see it beyond just our narrowed viewpoint. On one side of the building there may be a ladder that we need to get one person out of the building. We may have to go to the top of the building and then scaffold down to get someone else. This is why it's really important as we sort through our traumas to open up and look at things from a holistic perspective. Understanding that if we look at it from a view that has many perspectives, we'll be able to understand it from many perspectives.

Once we can see the complete picture, we get an entirely different view with various storylines we never considered. We might have told ourselves the story of what happened in one way. I mean, there's been many times in my life where I reflected on traumatic events, then spoke to the other people involved and asked for their perspectives. Not only in some cases did people tell me a totally different perspective, in many situations where multiple people were involved, they insisted the story didn't actually happen the way I perceived it.

Understand that the mind is a very tricky thing. We must be very careful because there are stories we tell ourselves about ourselves to feel better. In the process of making ourselves feel better, we can easily botch reality. Most times, we make the traumatic event even more traumatic than it was.

Taking a holistic perspective is a great way to bring new awareness to your traumas so healing can begin. Get different perspectives, dig a little deeper, and lean into the situation instead of walking away from it or sweeping it under the rug. It never feels good and sometimes is frightening to have to revisit something that scarred you. You'll find that being brave enough to heal is always worth it. And the good thing is, you don't have to walk that journey alone because therapy is therapeutic.

Remember, to adopt a holistic perspective involves looking at it from all perspectives which includes your personal views, the other person's views (attempting to step into their shoes), looking at it from a spiritual standpoint, as well as from a standpoint of, "How is this trauma serving me? How did this trauma damage me? What do I need to do about that damage?"

A holistic point-of-view looks to take a situation that has been chopped up and make it whole again.

We spend so much of our life blaming, deflecting, and shaming without ever achieving the peace we deserve. If we want different results, we have to be willing to think differently and be different. The idea of stepping out of our shoes to walk in someone else's, especially someone who might've hurt you, may seem repulsive and create anxiety. Remember, you're not doing it for them. This is all about you and your healing. And as ironic as it may seem, sometimes the person who hurt you (even if it's just stepping into their shoes) is part of your healing process.

Be willing to see the bigger picture to get the lesson life is teaching you. Forgiveness is a lesson. So is understanding. Either talk to the other person or people involved directly or get into therapy and allow the situation to be mapped out and talked about in more detail with a wider perspective. That's the first thing you can do.

Another thing you can do is adopt a thriver's mindset instead of a survivor's mindset. When you look at yourself as a survivor, you're looking at yourself from the perspective of 'I went through the situation and I survived it'. A survivor's mindset doesn't mean you actually conquered the situation. It just simply means the situation didn't kill you, which is still worth celebrating.

Taking on a thriver's mentality is a completely different way of thinking. A thriver's mentality means, 'I not only went through and survived my situation, but I became better as a result of the experience'. Thrivers confront what could possibly destroy them and end up discovering wisdom and a more evolved version of themselves. You are a thriver. Survival was the minimal requirement, but you wanted more.

You can look at it from the perspective of, 'I'm going to use this experience to inform my future self so I can overcome any obstacle that's similar or in the same lane as this one.'

In order to thrive and rise above your traumas, you must be willing to ask yourself, "How can this trauma actually be a part of my healing? How can it be a part of my expansion?"

If you've been operating in survivorship or victimhood for God knows how long, you might not even think it's possible or know the first place to begin removing your attachment to your pain.

The first thing you'll need to do is evaluate the predominant traumatic emotions that surface when you're thinking about the trauma itself or have similar situations that trigger you. For example, guilt usually comes from a lack of forgiveness. We feel guilt when we wrong others and we even blame ourselves when we're on the other end of the stick. Whenever we're in situations where we're unwilling to forgive someone, we're left holding the bag, so to speak. Because we end up having to deal with unresolved emotions of the experience by ourselves.

We can't leave these situations unaddressed because emotions like guilt are toxic. If left to fester, guilt will destroy you from the inside out. Forgiveness allows you to navigate the muddy waters of guilt. The first person you have to forgive is yourself because most people blame themselves, even in situations where it's 100% not their fault.

We have to learn to become more patient and gentle with ourselves. You're not perfect. No one is. Allow yourself the space to grow. Our minds are full of negative innuendo when it comes to the imperfections of others, and especially our own.

Be cognizant of the stories you tell yourself, especially around your traumas. Our traumas don't make us who we are. They are simply experiences that happened *FOR* us. How we respond to those traumas, how we allow those things to add meaning to our lives is what makes us who we are.

Remember, the things we tell ourselves are ultimately the things that create our identities. Most of us are defining ourselves by our imperfections, traumas, and the stories we tell ourselves, even if they're lies just to ease the pain.

Make sure there's accountability, acceptance, and forgiveness incorporated in the stories you tell yourself because you are ultimately the author of your stories, and those stories define you.

HOW TO GET UNSTUCK

As human beings, we've perfected the art of storytelling since the beginning of time. The stories we tell are often used to inspire, captivate, teach, and entertain anyone who will listen. Storytelling helps to conjure emotions, connection to others, creativity, communication, and imagination. We tend to lose ourselves in stories because they are far more entertaining embellishments of our actual reality.

The reality of our day-to-day lives doesn't satisfy us for some reason. Even before biblical times, the village storyteller would spice up folktales with supernatural and superstitious exaggerations to enhance the entertainment quality of the story. Today is no different. Movies and television tell a glossed-up version of reality. Even reality shows on television today aren't real. We are so disenchanted with our own lives, we'd rather create entertaining toxic versions of them to keep us amused.

The impact of social media alone on the human psyche in the last 15 years has been devastating. We log in for hours to scroll through the white-washed versions of people's daily lives. We then take a bite of the apple by comparing our "regular lives" to their photoshopped pictures, pretend happy moments, and disconnected baecations. It seems like everybody is catfishing.

Then, we take a dump on our own lives when we take the bait. Whether you swipe left or swipe right, there's a constant reminder that you're not enough and you don't have enough. Between commercials and social media, there's an endless flash of wads of cash, exotic cars, voluptuous bottoms, Gucci belts, and red bottoms pricking at our egos. We go from feeling like we're on top of the world to thinking we're scraping the bottom of the barrel.

This is the reason so many people hate their jobs, regret their relationships, and are saddened by what they've been able to achieve. It's because they're comparing their lives to what they see on Instagram. They never take the time to evaluate what they truly want for themselves, or if what they want is just the approval of strangers in the form of likes and emojis. Don't get me wrong, social media isn't all bad; it's brought the world together in ways it's never been connected. However, recent studies have confirmed a direct correlation between increased social media use and the risk of developing depression.

This is because the media and social media dissolve our connection with ourselves, which prevents us from appreciating what we do have. So, we end up living life in a zombie-like state. Hypnotized by everybody's life except our own. Waking up every day doing the same activities in the same sequence at some point will get redundant and feel robotic for anyone. The very essence of our human nature makes us crave variety, spontaneity, and progress. Every area of our lives is supposed to evolve and be a continuous flow of experiences, like a river. When that flow is disrupted, it's normal for us to feel boxed in, stagnant, and stuck.

Feeling stuck can make us feel paralyzed physically, mentally, and emotionally. We want to move, but we can't. So, we ultimately end up feeling trapped, anxious, and depressed because our natural disposition is to be free. Today, we're not bound by shackles or barriers of a caste system. We're bound by our own self-imposed limitations. It's those limitations that cause us to be boxed into hypnotic patterns that make us unhappy. According to a study, 69% of people feel trapped in an old, monotonous routine, while only 3 out of 10 people are actually happy with their lives.

Being stuck is like unknowingly stepping into quicksand. The more you struggle to get out, the deeper you'll sink.

Instead of fighting against an invisible bully, we should surrender. Relax. Realign. Refocus. Our need to control things beyond our control is based on hidden fears and insecurities. Resistance to the natural flow of life creates more struggle and suffering.

Whenever I come into contact with resistance, I see it as a sign to relax and surrender. It's definitely not a sign to do more of what I have been doing by working harder. It's delusional for us to keep doing the same thing and expect a new result. We have to step outside of the box to do and think differently.

Once we step outside the box, we often discover we're not as stuck as we think. We're just so fixated on the past and the future we can't be proactive in the present. Our attachment to the past and addiction to the future have us spellbound. We all want to unlock the possibilities of our full potential. But we have to get out of our own way to get things moving again. It's easy to feel hopeless when the past is dim because it often predicts a gloomy future; that doesn't mean it's the end. Feeling stuck is often a sign that it's time for new beginnings. However, in a hopeless state, we confuse a resurrection for an ending instead.

Remember, old keys can't open new doors.

We must be prepared to shut the doors on old situations before new opportunities will appear. I want to help you do this. But becoming unstuck isn't just about changing. You have to be willing to completely transform. Like the caterpillar accepts he must isolate inside of a cocoon in complete darkness for him to become a butterfly. It doesn't always feel good to make that kind of sacrifice, but he knows that's the only way he'll ever fly.

Are you willing to take a leap and grow wings on the way down? If so, I'll first tell you how we get stuck and then I'll give you a roadmap to becoming unstuck. Being stuck is a safe place in your comfort zone where nothing challenges you. Remember, you can't stay in the kiddie pool forever because nothing grows in your comfort zone.

The Most Common Ways We Get Stuck

- When we're unclear about what we want in life, it creates mixed messages about what we should be doing.

- Decision paralysis leads to over-analysis that creates procrastination. Nike said it best, "Yesterday, you said tomorrow. Just Do It."

- When we use our life circumstances as excuses, they become the greatest justification for inactivity.

- Not knowing thyself is the source of lack of self-belief. When you know your true self, it breeds confidence.

Most people know what they don't want through trial and error, but they don't know what they want because they don't know who they are.

- Contradicting beliefs create misalignments that keep you stuck. You can't believe because you grew up poor, you'll always be poor but also believe you'll become rich. Align your beliefs with your desires.

- Comparison is the thief of joy. The minute we compare ourselves to others, it shifts our focus from what we have to what we don't have. This triggers feelings of inferiority that lowers your self-esteem. Our joy comes from having gratitude for the blessings we already have.

Now that we've discussed some of the most common ways we get stuck in life, it's only right I show you the ways to become unstuck. Simply learning what got you stuck won't get you unstuck. But, it is very useful for your own personal transformation. The two go hand-in-hand. Evolution is a journey with no destination. So, focus on progression, not perfection.

How To Get Unstuck

- Discover your why. Until you discover your why (purpose), how and what will be insignificant. It's imperative you know your why, reason, passion, purpose, etc., before any shift in your life can happen for you.

- Be your authentic self. So many of us compare ourselves to others and pretend to be someone we're not because we don't understand how powerful and unique it is to be who we were born to be. Take off the mask and show the world who you are. That is your superpower. "You're a one-of-one. That means none before it, none to come." - Jay Z

- Show up for yourself. Most of being successful is about showing up. You can't win if you're not present. Show up and show out even if no one claps or shows up except you.

- Change your inner dialogue. Did you know that 87% of our self-talk, or the dialogue we have with ourselves, is negative? Only listen to the voice that's rooting for you. Don't argue with the one that isn't. "Whatever you give your attention to grows." - Joseph Murphy

- Eliminate self-sabotage. This means you must get out of your own way. An old African Proverb states: "If there's no enemy within, there can be no enemy without." Be aware of old habits and thinking that no longer serve you.

- Redefine success. There is no cookie-cutter definition of what success is. Success is something you must define for yourself based on your terms and the desires in your heart. When you create the standards for what success is for you, only you can determine whether or not you're successful. You no longer have to be a slave to societal norms or someone else's approval to validate your achievements.

- Eliminate the need to be perfect. Focus on progression, not perfection. There's not a desire worth having that would require you to be perfect. Our imperfections make us human and help us grow.

- Create routines that breed progression. Small steps will get you anywhere you need to go. Incorporate routines like daily goal setting, meditation for clarity, and reading daily for personal development to ensure you're always shifting outside the box.

- If needed, find an accountability partner. We were not made to be alone. So, find someone in your life who is rooting for you and wants to see you win. Hold each other accountable for getting unstuck and staying that way.

Strive to be completely transformed, not just changed. The unfortunate downside of change is we can always revert back to old behaviors. Once transformed, there's nothing left behind to change back to. All the old versions of yourself will become evolved, too. This will liberate you from your past so your present can claim whatever future you desire.

Getting unstuck makes us feel whole again. This allows us to become more connected with our true selves instead of a facade. That's when all the real magic happens. Your intuition will be loud and clear. Your faith will be stronger than ever. You'll have clarity about your purpose that allows you to move mountains.

HOW TO GET YOUR SHIFT GOING

I mentioned in the previous chapter how easy it is to get stuck in life. It happens so quickly you don't even know how you got there. But once you know why you got stuck and how to get unstuck, the focus becomes how to get shift going.

Getting unstuck is like pushing a car out of the mud. Now, it's time to shift into gear and get moving.

Shifting in life is where purpose and meaning meet a massive amount of focus and determination. A shift is a break in the pattern of redundancy and stagnancy that leads to a turning point. When we create a shift in our lives, our motivation now comes from our divine purpose and our desperate need to impact the world we live in. Our calling, so to speak.

We all want to know that our life has meaning and that our existence plays a role in the grand design. Being used as a vessel for divine purpose provides the greatest sense of meaning for life.

I believe we all are born with seeds of divine purpose planted in our hearts by God. This is where I believe the phrase "follow your heart" comes from. It's our responsibility to water and facilitate the growth of the seeds throughout our life journey. The things in our hearts that ignite our passions and set our souls on fire are like GPS signals for identifying our purposes in life. When we walk away from our purposes and passions, we walk away from the most authentic versions of ourselves. This is why so many people feel lost.

Shift is simply moving in the direction that helps you rediscover yourself and the garden of seeds you have stored in your heart. This allows you to live a purpose-driven and fulfilled life. To do this, you must reconnect with your heart.

Society, and even the people we love, teach us to deny the things in our hearts and embrace rational socially accepted standards. They tell us to be an accountant when it's obvious we hate numbers. To become a doctor even when they know you love to paint. And we're punished for being class clowns when we feel most inspired by making others laugh and smile.

In business, they say if you want to find the cause of something, follow the money. Well, if you want to find the meaning of life, follow purpose. Those tiny seeds that have been nudging you your entire life are breadcrumbs to discovering what your purpose in life is. They are the things that come naturally for you and not for others. They are the things that attract others to you and even you to yourself. It's a talent or skill you would gladly share even if you didn't get paid for it.

"If you do what you love and love what you do, you'll never work a day in your life." It always sounded like a good philosophy, but it wasn't until I got shift going by aligning myself with my purpose that I fully understood it. Once I started living on purpose, my work didn't feel like work anymore. It felt like an adventure. I could work 16 hours in a day and still have enough energy to keep pushing.

When I worked in the hospital, I enjoyed being a clinician, but didn't enjoy my work. By the end of my work shift every day, I felt like I needed a vacation. I was doing what I wanted to do by being in healthcare, but not doing it how I felt I should do it. So, whenever I got a chance to speak to a group of friends or at a local event or church in a way that resonated with me, I did. This kept me inspired and showed me what my purpose was. Most of the time I was speaking, it didn't even feel like it was coming from me. It felt like it was coming through me, being downloaded from a higher consciousness. It sparked a light in me that others saw and that I recognized, too.

This created the proverbial fork in the road we all eventually come to. Am I going to take the road less traveled and live on purpose or continue down the path of conformity and rationality?

I deviated and took the road less traveled. Let me tell you why. If I took the path that made more sense, I'd feel safer and it would feel like the more intelligent decision. Sadly, in the end, I would live an unfulfilled life; ultimately, an empty life. The last thing I want to do is look back on my life in my twilight years and think about what could've or should've been. So many dreams and beautiful ideas are buried in the graveyard, never having been shared with the world. I don't want to take any of my greatness to the grave. I want to leave it all on the table or at least die trying to get it all out.

Most of us spend our entire lives failing miserably at something we don't want to do. Why not be fulfilled and do something we love? And that's exactly what I ended up doing, firing my job and walking out on faith.

Now I'll be the first to tell you, I worried constantly about where money would come from. I was nervous about the lack of security that came with being unemployed and often wondered how foolish my colleagues believed I was for throwing away my career. I kept telling myself, "Do what you love and love what you do."

I don't know what your hopes and dreams are, but I do know there is a calling inside all of us. What we often perceive as barriers to discovering that calling are actual individual bricks laid down on your path to build the foundation for your own self-actualization. Every brick is preparing you for the ultimate shift you want to occur in life.

Don't walk away or around it, lean into the discomfort. When you feel nudged by something that ignites you, go in that direction.

Even if you don't yet believe in yourself, remember my story. I'm living proof. If you're willing to be obedient to the whispers of your calling and accept every experience as preparation whether good or bad, nothing is impossible for you.

The very word impossible can be transformed into "I'M POSSIBLE."

ABUNDANCE IS YOUR DIVINE INHERITANCE

I believe all of humanity is in the process of making a tremendous shift in consciousness. That shift is going to change how we view and relate to each other, ourselves, and the world. This new consciousness will allow us to have a greater understanding of what we are capable of once we become self-actualized.

We'll realize that our limitations are self-imposed and most often passed down by society on to our parents then on to us. Removing these shackles will ultimately reveal poverty isn't just a socioeconomic status but a state of mind that can be shifted to change our circumstances.

Our understanding of abundance, how it's created and accumulated is so misguided, it keeps us grounded in poverty.

Therefore, we have to first redefine what abundance is and the source of its creation before we can ever accumulate anything of value and actually appreciate it.

So, let's start there. There are a lot of myths about abundance, many with a negative connotation. Some people believe poverty is part of the divine plan. I do not believe that poverty is God's will. We were made in God's image and from divine essence. By default, this makes us ALL creators. We all have the ability to be abundant.

Another common misperception about abundance is that it only includes material wealth. I believe the richness of abundance should be present in our relationships, health, thinking, experiences, spirituality, love, compassion, goals, and material wealth. Most of us were taught to eat humble pie when it comes to abundance. We end up denying ourselves of what we're all privy to because of ideas like "money is the root of all evil." Society, and even those we love, pound these untruths into us from the day we're born. Money itself is not evil; it's what we choose to do with money and what we're willing to do for money. When we allow money to change us for the worse, that's what makes it evil.

Another one of the biggest misconceptions about abundance is that it comes from outside of us. Most people believe wealth is something that can only be obtained externally. However, the truth is every aspect of abundance you're seeking comes from within you.

This is the very reason so many people spend most of their lives chasing money. Our education and our upbringing have taught us that wealth is tangible and material; contrarily, our greatest wealth lies within us.

Chasing money is the rat race we've all taken part in. We chase money in exchange for time, status, approval, and materialism. Here's a secret very few people know, **YOU ARE THE MONEY**.

Stop chasing dollars. That's a race you'll never win.

Abundance is the infinite cycle of receiving and giving. It begins by giving your thoughts, time, effort, and relentless faith. Then ultimately, the law of attraction returns the favor several times over. The law of attraction is beautifully described in the book, *Ask and It Is Given*, by Esther and Jerry Hicks.

The best example I have to describe the law of attraction is the relationship between Aladdin and the Genie. Like Aladdin, it is our job to figure out what we want and wish for. The Genie plays the role of the Universe waiting for us to rub the lamp three times and express our wishes. The three rubs are to get the attention of the Universe and each rub represents our thoughts, feelings, and the words we speak.

Thoughts are the highest vibrational frequency we can send out to the Universe. Aligning all our thoughts with our desires (wishes) sends the loudest and most noticeable signal. For instance, if you desire to be wealthy, every thought whether conscious or subconscious, must be in alignment with you being wealthy NOW before you can attract it to you in reality.

It doesn't matter that you don't currently have the material wealth to prove it. What's important is that you think you have a wealth of knowledge and resources, and desire to attract wealth in your direction as you draw it to you like a magnet. Let me be clear. Nothing outside of you can affect what you attract unless you invite it into your creative process. So, if you believe someone else's negativity towards you is binding, then it will be.

The next highest vibrational frequency are the feelings we send out into the Universe. Our thoughts create our feelings. Once our thoughts are in alignment, we must feel as though we've already received what we've asked for. It's almost impossible to attract being lean and fit when you feel fat. You may indeed still have a tremendous amount of excess body weight but feeling fat only creates negative feelings like shame. Getting fit mindfully and emotionally puts you in a mindset to exercise, eat well, and it sends signals to every cell in your body that being lean and fit is actually happening.

Shame will always keep you stuck in life. To be clear, I'm not asking you to pretend like you're thin. This will only create a feeling of being inauthentic and delusional. What I'm suggesting is that you imagine what a leaner and fitter version of you feels and looks like. What would it feel like to look in your mirror and see a chiseled version of yourself? How would you feel to slip into a pair of jeans several sizes smaller? How would it feel exercising as a healthier version of you? What would it feel like to know you've added a tremendous amount of health and longevity to your life? How would it feel to know you've inspired other people you care about to do the same thing?

Those types of feelings are genuinely authentic. They change how you feel about yourself and what is attracted to you. Our feelings are our GPS navigational system. It's important we get in tune with our intuition to decipher whether those feelings are coming from a place of authenticity, from fear, or our egos.

The next thing we can do to get our genie to appear is to only use powerful words that attract what we want. It has always been said that there is power in the tongue. It's capable of building or destroying ourselves and those around us.

Did you know the word "Abracadabra" often used by magicians before they displayed a magic trick is Hebrew? It's taken from three words "ab" (father), "ben" (son), and "ruach hakodesh" (holy spirit) and corruption of the Hebrew phrase "ebrah k'dabri", meaning "I will create as I speak or I will have what I say."

Magicians like Houdini knew the power of words and so should you.

The words you speak and listen to create a vibrational frequency that will return its equivalent match. This means the words you speak, the conversations you're a part of, and the music you listen to will affect what you attract. If you speak down about others and take part in gossip that will become a part of your reality on the opposite end. This is a universal law. It happens by default whether you want it to or not.

Not watching the news and listening to certain genres of music are just a few ways I protect my energy and keep my positivity. Most importantly, I speak life into myself and others. And in the rare case where I find it difficult to speak positively about someone, I give them love and send them on their way.

Our task is to be a relentless gatekeeper of the words we speak and the inner dialogue that takes place within us. The conversations we have within us are just as important as the ones we have with others. As I said before, 87% of our internal conversation is negative. Much of the internal dialogue we're having is on repeat. Telling us we're not enough, what we can't do, how unworthy we are, and creating stories that prevent us from being our authentic selves.

Most of this is coming from our subconscious programming that was established by the time we were in 2nd grade. We can't change what happened to us then, but we can change the programming we learned by constantly interrupting those conversations and replacing them with words of empowerment. Eventually, what we say out in the world and what we say to ourselves will align with our deepest desires and we'll see our own words come to fruition.

There is a fourth rub that helps to get the attention of the Universe to conspire in your favor, but it's the lowest vibrational signal and that is action.

I highly recommend you get your thoughts, feelings, and words in alignment before you take any action. Attempting to take action before finding alignment is like jumping in a car to start your journey without fuel, tires, or a steering wheel. It creates an unnecessary uphill battle. Is it possible to still make it? Yes. However, by aligning ourselves first, we create the least amount of resistance on our path.

The other important benefit of being in alignment is it helps us reclaim our time back. Time, not money, is the true currency of life and it's indispensable. We cannot replace it. Most of us spend the first 20 years of our lives in primary and secondary school. Then, the next 45 years are spent working for a company that will never fully compensate us for our true value. We hope it will at least lead to a sustainable retirement.

What we never think about is how work plays into the grand scheme of life. The average life expectancy in the United States is now 76 years. That gives us roughly ten years to enjoy life in retirement, if healthy enough to do so. If it sounds like a rip-off, that's because it is. Think about it like this, if I told you to give me $45 and I would give you $10 in exchange, you would think I was a damn fool. But we sign up for this deal every day because we never tap into our own ability to create abundance. We exchange our time for dollars and agree to wait two weeks and sometimes a month to be compensated for it.

The generations before us taught us that the only way to abundance is to earn and save our way to freedom. And this model may have been perfect for the generations before us that didn't have thousands of dollars in student loan debt and medical bills. Add 40 years of inflation and the exponential jump in the cost of living as a cherry on top, and we see that their model of abundance is just as inappropriate as dial-up internet is for video streaming.

We must shift our mindset from poverty-based thinking that has convinced us scarcity is rampant and there's not enough for everyone to live a good life. We are constantly being told money doesn't grow on trees, yet they're printing it by the trillions every day.

Everything we need and most of what we want is easily supplied by nature. Food, water, sunshine, fresh air, clothing, shelter, and even more can easily be supplied to every man, woman, and child without scratching a zero off nature's bank account. Even the iPhone requires cobalt taken from the soil of the Democratic Republic of Congo.

When we look at nature closely enough, we find it infinitely produces in abundance. Here's an example: the first mango tree in existence sprouted from a single seed. That same tree grew and eventually produced an abundance of mangoes. Animals that came along and ate the mangoes spread the seed by taking it back to their homes and dropping the leftover seeds to the ground when they finished eating. Those seeds sank in the soil and sometime later more mango trees grew.

Humans came along and traveled even greater distances, spreading the seed even further. Now mango trees grow wherever the environment is conducive for them to do so. Whenever a mango falls to the ground and isn't eaten, it nourishes the soil, which makes the tree produce even more mangoes. This is life and how abundance works, all from a single seed and nothing is wasted.

We don't view our lives this way because we've been programmed to think there are exceptions to the rules.

An example of this programming can be illustrated by the company De Beers Diamonds. They convinced us diamonds are rare and forever. What we didn't know was diamonds haven't been rare since 1870, when a huge diamond mine was discovered in South Africa. Many other mines have popped up since. The Venetia mine in South Africa produces about 4 million carats annually.

Diamonds have no intrinsic value. Their value is solely based on false scarcity created by mining companies cornering the marketing and controlling supply and demand. By the way, Russia has at least three mines larger than the one in South Africa. Diamonds essentially have the equivalent monetary value of crystal quartz or cubic zirconia.

Nature, outside of us and within us, provides everything we need in abundance. The Jedi mind trick they play is to convince us otherwise for their fortune at our own expense.

In the same way, they convinced us pharmaceutical drugs were a replacement for using food as medicine as the foundation for health. No drug actually keeps you healthy. What it does is manipulate your biochemistry to keep you from getting sicker (which can be very useful but it's not a cure).

Nutritious food combined with a healthy lifestyle creates abundant health. Whereas prescription drugs can only be prescribed when you've been diagnosed as sick. Most people are shocked to find out that at one point over half of the drugs on the market were just synthetic knockoffs of plant-based derivatives. It was often well-known that the plant outperformed the prescription drug.

It's time we pull back the veil and shift our mindset back into alignment with being a co-creator with the Universe.

The first step is to shift your mind because what you say, do, and feel are just extensions of what you're thinking. So, what you think will ultimately create your experiences in life. Therefore, when we change our thoughts, we ultimately end up changing our lives.

The harder and longer you think about anything, the stronger the attraction you'll receive from the Universe. It's like the moment you decide you want a certain car you rarely see, suddenly you see that car everywhere. That's the law of attraction at work. It reflects your thoughts back to you. It's also true that if your predominant thoughts are scarcity, negativity, and lack, those things will also be reflected back to you through your life experiences.

It's this lack of understanding that creates so much chaos in our lives. Because we don't understand how our life experiences are being created, we end up creating by default instead of through intentionality. We see life as random and chaotic because our thoughts are random and chaotic. This is also why we falsely believe other people have control over the outcomes of our lives, because we don't understand how creation and abundance works.

No one can put a hex on you or create ill will in your life unless you empower their thoughts by making them your own.

In closing, I want to give you a few reminders to help you as you set out on a new path of living life more abundantly.

Tips for Living More Abundantly

- Know exactly what you want. Typically, if I ask someone what they want out of life, they'll start stuttering. Conversely, if I ask them what they don't want, they have a complete laundry list of items they start spouting off endlessly.

- Get a very clear vision about what you want for your life. Remember whenever you are unclear on what you want, what you receive in life will appear just as fuzzy. Most importantly, when you don't create with intention, you'll still manifest your life experiences by whatever default thinking that is present.

- Develop an attitude of gratitude that aligns you with the Source from which all abundance comes. We must learn to appreciate what we have before any other blessings will be given to us. How can you be happy with more when you aren't satisfied with what you have? Everything you've accumulated at this point was preparation for the next upgrade. Take your mind off the destination and learn to appreciate every step of the journey. An attitude of gratitude is akin to an abundant mindset.

Jim Carrey said, "I wish everyone could get rich and famous and have everything they ever dreamed of so they can see that that's not the answer."

He's not saying that abundance won't serve you. He's saying it won't fulfill you if you don't appreciate life. Be grateful for what you have and keep that same energy for all your desires as if you already received them.

- Another huge tip is giving. Giving is just as much part of abundance as receiving. Abundance is a beautiful cycle of reaping and sowing. That flow becomes disrupted when we choose to hoard the wealth we receive from Source. Not giving comes from a poverty mindset. Even the rich often suffer from this. Eventually, their wealth will be reduced to ashes. In addition, hoarding and calling it savings for rainy days will only create more rainy days (because the Universe returns the thought you think several times fold).

Remember you can always give no matter how much you have because it doesn't have to be money. Knowledge and kindness are often far more valuable than a monetary donation. I would much rather teach a man or woman how to fish as they say, rather than give them fish. Be sure to make regular giving a part of your abundance practice.

- The next tip is money is a terrible master but an excellent servant. Most of what we've been taught about money is often the opposite of what we should have learned. We were all taught that working hard for our money creates a great sense of pride, but to create abundance we have to make our money work for us. The great thing about money is that it is a tireless servant. It doesn't need sleep, repayment, food, or appreciation. It just needs to be put to work.

When money doesn't have work to do, it is simply waiting to be spent. A rainy day for those that only save and never invest is always a day away. Invest in yourself, the stock market, real estate, a new business, bitcoin, NFTs, or whatever you feel most comfortable and capable of doing.

In the book, *The Richest Man in Babylon*, it says, "Learn to make your treasure work for you. Make it your slave. Make its children, and its children's children, work for you." I don't care how hard and long you work, you will never be able to outwork your money. Always take a portion of your money and reinvest it to multiply your riches. Make sure you make intelligent decisions and use expert counsel when you invest.

Just don't allow money to master you by shackling you in the new form of enslavement known as debt.

Lastly, I don't want to have you under the impression that you should lay in your bed thinking, speaking, and feeling your way into abundance, especially men. The feminine energy that women naturally have makes them natural multipliers.

Generally speaking, women are more in tune with nature. As a result, manifesting comes much easier for them. This definitely doesn't mean men can't manifest abundance through the law of attraction because we can, and we do. However, work or action in our current state of consciousness is the vibrational frequency most men are familiar with, so effort is required to get shift going. Especially if you ever feel like things are stuck.

In addition, if you don't feel moved or inspired to work tirelessly on what you want, it's probably an indication that it's not something within your divine purpose.

When you go after something that's aligned with your purpose, you'll be so obsessed that even a back-breaking effort won't feel like work. Because as I stated before "when we love what we do and do what we love, we never work a day in our lives."

Embrace your ability to create the abundance you want not just with money. Embrace abundant health, love, happiness, thinking, expansion and in every other area of your life.

TAKE A LEAP & GROW WINGS

When was the last time you did something for the first time? What I'm really asking in this question is how often do you step outside of your box. Do you ever walk to the outer edges of your capabilities and push? Or do you like to remain comfortably snuggled up in your comfort zone?

It's so easy for us to remain inside the boundaries of what's comfortable for us. It's safe, we feel secure, and we always know what to expect. This is why so many of us remain in unhealthy relationships and work at jobs we hate. We don't want to go through the necessary discomfort required to stretch ourselves.

The truth is, we were all made to be stretched far beyond what we think we're capable of. Throughout our lives, there are pivotal moments where we come face-to-face with the option to either take a leap or remain grounded. Most of us will walk to the edge, look over, then turn back around in fear. The fear comes from choosing to only focus on what could go wrong instead of the magic we could create from a leap of faith. We call it a leap of faith because our choice goes against reason and embraces a hope we have in our hearts. It's spontaneous and uncalculated like a shot in the dark.

I've always been in love with the recklessness of taking a leap of faith. It always felt like a win-win instead of simply not having anything to lose. From my perspective, I was either choosing to be the author of my own real-life adventure or allowing life to dictate how the next chapter of my story would go. We come to this fork in the road in so many aspects of life: job opportunities in another country, breakup or makeup, starting a new business, telling someone you love them, or forgiving someone who hurt you. These are just a few of the heroic moments we overlook and downplay in our day-to-day lives.

All these moments can change the trajectories of our lives. That's exactly what they're designed to do. This is what makes us so powerful. We have the ability to choose what's next, how we will respond, and what we desire. Most people don't see the power to choose as a gift, so they run from it like a curse. I've seen people faced with something as simple as choosing what to eat go into instant decision paralysis. As a result, they end up staying in their safety box and eating what they always eat.

How many times have you done this in various aspects of your life?

Stayed in a relationship too long because the idea of having to get back on the dating market and sifting through the endless number of choices and potential failures on Tinder horrified you. Procrastinated on starting the business you've always dreamed about because the security of a bi-weekly check keeps you nice and cozy like a warm blanket. Never writing the book you always dreamed about because of your fear of being critiqued or thought of as an imposter. Every decision we make and choose not to make impacts our lives.

Yes, indecision is a decision.

When we make choices that set our souls on fire and inspire us to act, we empower ourselves. When we remove ourselves from the decision-making process and become silent on the matters that will most impact our lives, we take part in one of the greatest self-inflicted injustices. This is exactly what was being called out with white liberals and hipsters during the George Floyd protest.

Black and brown people like myself saw their white liberal friends being silent at work, on social media, and even in the presence of their racist friends and family members as President 45 poured gasoline on the fires of racism across the country. We reminded them that choosing not to say anything was a decision to embrace the same "White Privilege" that allowed a white police officer to kneel on a hand-cuffed black man's neck for eight minutes and forty-six seconds pressed against the concrete on a hot summer's day until all the life was squeezed out of him.

Dr. Martin Luther King said, "Our lives begin to end the day we become silent about the things that matter." His focus was injustice, but I want to inspire you to be loud and passionate about all matters of your life. Don't be afraid to take a leap of faith and grow wings on the way down. Our greatest adventures will always come when we step into the unknown. No bird learns to fly on the ground. They jump with no practice, only a belief that this is what I was born to do.

Our domestication and love for being inside boxes prevents us from flying. Like the modern chicken that lost its ability to fly due to being caged and weighed down by the farmer's chicken feed, instead of its natural diet. If we want to fly, we have to leave the box and take a leap. The leap is our faith (leap = faith). Believing in something that has not yet been realized. Our faith is what will lead us to the hidden treasures in our lives. Whenever we take a leap, it creates momentum, and that's what gets shift going.

The wings we build on the way down are self-belief. Taking a leap teaches us to trust and believe in ourselves. The opposite of what society tells us to do. We're so focused on trying to do the "right" thing that we forget to listen to our intuition. Intuition is communication from our higher selves. It consists of downloads we receive from the spiritual plane as guidance towards our own self-expansion. The more we ignore it, the fainter the signal becomes. Intuition is like a muscle. The more you use it, the more it grows. Trusting your intuition is trusting your higher self. We must build this trust within ourselves in order to grow our wings.

It's imperative for us to know that we're capable of doing "it" before we actually do it. The philosopher Young Jeezy said, "You can't sell it until you buy it." In other words, if you don't believe it why should anyone else? You have to see it before you believe it. Not physically see it with your two eyes, but with the vision you have for your life. Growing your wings on the way down encourages YOU to bet on YOU. I know taking a leap without wings is scary. The wind and gravity remind you how devastating the fall could be if you don't succeed. The fear of pain and failure will try to consume you. Keep in mind, without pressure, not even diamonds could be formed.

Don't allow fear to disempower you. Move boldly toward your desires with courage. Yes, I said courage. Having courage isn't the absence of fear, it's pressing forward despite your fears. Like diving into a deep abyss not knowing how to swim but within arm's reach of a lifesaver. That's actually one of the many leaps I took in my life.

In 2017, I traveled to the Maldives to get a firsthand experience of what appeared to be a paradise island. I had spent the last six months in India practicing yoga and meditation, and taking bucket baths. I was excited about treating myself to a taste of luxury. The Maldives is a string of tropical islands in the Indian Ocean surrounded by turquoise blue lagoons and pure white sandy beaches. 99% of the Maldives landmass is covered by the sea.

This was a fact that I was unaware of prior to landing. The reason this was a point of interest is because I had always had a fear of water. Especially the kind of water that has waves and predatory creatures like sharks.

When I was a small child, my father would take me everywhere with him. In his late twenties, we went to hang out with some of his friends at a local creek. I watched in awe as they swung off ropes tied to tree branches and dived into the murky waters. With each swing getting more daring, you could hear a collective "boom" each time someone hit the water.

I was only four or five, so I don't remember my train of thought, but I'm sure I just got bored sitting on the sidelines and wanted to join the fun. So, I did. I held my breath, jumped in, and began to sink. I don't remember being worried. Shortly after I hit the water, my father dove in and pulled me back to safety. Needless to say, the fun was over for that day. I got scolded by my father for the rest of the day and it left an imprint on me. As a result, I never really learned to swim opting to stay on the kiddie end of the pool even as an adult.

Decades later, there I was in the middle of the Indian Ocean surrounded by water. Beautiful things sometimes have a way of stripping you of fear and arming you with bravery. That held true for me, especially with nature. Another interesting fact I learned on the boat ride from the airport was the resort itself was the island. When we docked, you could see the endless ocean in every direction. I took a moment to enjoy my over-water villa, then headed out to dip my feet into the ocean and find out what services were available through the resort.

Now because this resort was pretty fancy-schmancy, a lot of the activities were actually complimentary. Most of the activities were water sports. I love free! So, I took advantage of everything.

Paddle boarding, kayaking, etc. All with a life jacket securely fit, of course. The next morning, I received a call from a scuba diving instructor.

"I noticed you didn't take advantage of your complimentary scuba diving lesson. Would you like for us to make an appointment for you today?"

I quickly replied, "Oh no, I can barely swim. I skipped that one intentionally."

"I've been a master diver for over 30 years. I could give you some pointers on swimming and the complimentary session is only in 10 to 12 feet of water. You'll have a mask and oxygen tank, so you don't have to be a skilled swimmer."

To this day, I don't know why I said yes, but I did.

When I arrived, we must've gone through at least two hours of training before we ever touched the water. As soon as we did, every fear of water I had, emerged. The tank felt like a bag of cement on my back. Nowhere in my rationale would it allow me to believe it was possible to do anything besides sink like I did in that creek as a little boy. The instructor kept nudging me and assuring me that wouldn't be the case. I pushed forward because I didn't want to live in this fear anymore. For so long, I told myself I was too heavy and that my muscles were too dense, which is what made me a poor swimmer (these claims were totally unsubstantiated). The thought that got me into the water was I had seen divers float and swim, so why couldn't I?

I've always used that train of thinking to push beyond what I believe is possible for me. What's available for one is available for all.

What made it easier was seeing a huge, muscular German guy in the group just as cautious as I was. That gave me a little more comfort. After overcoming my initial anxiety, the underwater training felt pretty amazing. I learned how to remove water that seeped into the face mask while remaining underwater, how to expel water from the regulator mouthpiece, proper breathing techniques, how to inflate and deflate the lungs to either sink deeper or rise in the water, and so much more.

After we emerged from the water, the instructor complimented me on my ability to control my breath and inflate/deflate my lungs. Thinking back on it, all my yoga and meditation training in India had prepared me to do that.

It's amazing how our previous life experiences seem to always prepare us for what is to come. After he complimented me, he said, "Let's sign you up for the diving certification, my friend. You are a diver!"

I replied enthusiastically, "Let's do it!"

"All we need to do is go on two more dives in the open ocean."

I quickly shouted, "Oh no!"

We went back and forth about it for a bit. Eventually, I told him let me sleep on it.

I woke up early the next morning to watch the sunrise illuminate the sea. A phone call from the diving center broke the moment, "Are you ready for your scheduled dive today?" a lady asked.

"Let's do it."

The first dive was going to be exploring the coral reef between ten and twenty feet.

Once I zipped up my wet suit and strapped on my scuba tank, the weight of it all created a collage of fear-mongering news clips running across my mind. "Renowned pharmacist, Dr. Bobby Price, drowns in the Maldives while exploring the world." Thankfully, I remembered one thing the scuba instructor said.

"Most people who fear water end up drowning themselves and their saving grace lifeguard because they pull the lifeguard down with them. Being calm reduces the likelihood of incidents and makes solving problems easier." Message received.

I wanted to fall backwards into the water like I'd seen scuba divers do on television; but, I wasn't that brave yet. I crawled out of the boat into the water like a toddler leaving its crib.

As soon as I hit the water, panic set in. I quickly worked on regaining my composure by focusing on my breath. Once the instructor entered the water, I was ready and together we went under. As we descended, working our way around the coral reef, I could see a rainbow of colors. Hues of blues, greens, pink, and purple I had never seen before. There were colonies of fish, sponges, sea turtles, sea anemones, shellfish, and creatures I couldn't identify. I got so lost in the moment, I didn't realize an hour had gone by and it was time to go back up.

With scuba diving, you must be very careful about ascending too quickly. The night before at dinner, I saw a man who was at the diving center the first day I arrived. His eye was bloodshot red and he couldn't talk because a vein had burst in his neck. He had mistakenly ascended too quickly and paid a huge price. It scared the shit out of me because he was lively and friendly the first time we met. He'd become silent and pitiful.

I decided to take all the time I needed. By the time everyone else was back in the boat, I was still 12 feet under. Being able to control my breath and buoyancy like that really instilled a lot of confidence in me.

Once I was back in the boat, we all high-fived and talked about what we had seen in the underwater jungle. I was so high on the experience, I was now looking forward to the final dive the next day. The final dive was going to be 20 meters. That's the height of six and a half NBA regulation basketball rims stacked on top of each other. Up to this point I hadn't been on the side of the pool that was ten feet deep. After what I experienced that day, I opened up to taking another leap.

The next day we sailed out on the open water as the instructor explained the objectives of the final dive. Once we exited the boat, we would dive down slowly to 20 meters. At that point, we'd begin swimming a mile out from the boat. I asked how long that would be considering how much oxygen we had in our tanks and we'd ultimately have to swim back. His response informed me we'd be heading back much faster on a current. I obviously didn't know what that meant at the time. I just gave him a thumbs up and kept it moving.

We dove into the water and descended like the day before. It felt like we were scaling down a mountain and disappearing into the abyss. Every time I felt like the bottom of the ocean would appear out of the darkness, the blackness just kept reappearing. When we finally reached our target depth, the instructor used one sign he taught us to tell us to remain calm.

Initially, this was confusing because I was already calm. But then he pointed upwards. I quickly saw the dark figure slowly pacing across the water. It was a 10 to 12-foot great white shark.

Everything in me wanted to jump out of the water. But being 20 meters or better below the surface, I realized it wasn't possible. I became a floating statue. The shark moved on as if he was already full or wasn't interested in human fare at that moment. I spent the next 20 minutes looking over and around my shoulder as if we had narrowly escaped a drive-by.

We eventually came to the point where it was time to "enter" the current for our ride back to the boat. I had never seen the movie *Finding Nemo*, though I wish I had. The only instructions I received regarding the current was to control my breath to stay inside the current, otherwise I'd have to swim back. I was confident about controlling my breath, so I guess I overlooked the rest of the conversation.

I watched the instructor give my friend a boost into the current and they went in as if it had beamed them into a spaceship. We quickly followed. It was then that I finally realized what a current was. We were traveling what seemed to be 50 to 60 miles per hour. The only thing keeping us in the current was controlling the breath in our lungs. I watched the instructor pull a few of the other students down as they ascended out of the current. The moment was so surreal for me. It felt like a scene out of a sci-fi film.

We blazed through the water like human submarines. But everything had slowed down for me mentally. If you had told me 72 hours before that I would be 66 feet below the surface in the middle of an ocean watching man-eating sharks and gigantic sea turtles swim by as if we were neighbors and riding a current just slightly below the highway speed limit, I would've thought you were delusional. However, there I was, not only doing that in exact detail but enjoying every moment.

The next day, the diving instructor brought my scuba certification to the room and hugged me like a proud father.

I honestly didn't know I had it in me. I was okay just going to the Maldives, getting waist-deep in the water, and taking some dope photos. Instead, I had just taken a leap that crushed a lifelong fear. I wondered what other fears were just waiting for me to lean in and reveal the truth, and what other potential possibilities were those fears secretly keeping me from.

Now, ask yourself the same questions. Are you willing to leave the stuckness of yesterday behind in exchange for tomorrow's greatness?

If you are, then take a deep breath and leap off of your tallest fear to grow your own wings. Leap into the arms of your hopes and dreams and watch them embrace you as if they've always been waiting for you. Because they have.

CONCLUSION

Writing this book was easily one of the most difficult things I've ever done in my storied life. The entire process felt like peeling back scabs on old wounds and diving back into past traumas I had already healed from. No one likes to take a stroll down Traumas and Dramas Lane; but, these experiences are part of who we are. They don't define us unless we allow them to, yet they can remind us of how far we've come. Every page I wrote reminded me of the strength and power that comes from vulnerability. I was always told being vulnerable was a sign of weakness, so I hid my heartbreaks, held back my tears, suppressed expressing my fears, and tried to pretend like my failures never happened.

I hope by reading this book you will have an expanded perspective not only on the things to come, but also on the experiences you had in the past. Tragic or triumphant, our experiences are small treasures of wisdom waiting to be discovered. The five senses we commonly use to interpret life are not enough to see what's truly there. We have to go beyond our narrow-minded thinking to see the bigger picture and tap into our multi-sensory capabilities.

One of my favorite quotes by Muhammad Ali is, "A man who views the world the same way at 50 as he did when he was 20 has wasted 30 years of his life." The quote reminds us that life is about evolving and expanding our perspectives. It doesn't say we should've accumulated this or accomplished that. It simply states that our views on life must expand by pulling the wisdom out of our own life experiences.

When we allow life itself to become our guru, we get a divine teacher who can be hard but fair. 'Guru' is a Sanskrit term known in eastern philosophy as a spiritual teacher or one who imparts initiation.

The initiation we're having is our human experience as a spiritual being. The primary purpose of our human experience is a rite of passage. Which is essentially a collection of ritual activities (life experiences) and teachings (life lessons) designed to strip the individual of the layers of a false self, created by society and reestablish karmic balance. The sole purpose of this process is to prepare us for becoming higher versions of ourselves. What's important to note is that we play an active role in developing the curriculum of the experiences we go through before ever being born. This is why I say life isn't happening to you, it's happening for you.

It was your spirit that decided who your parents would be, whether you would be popular, who you would fall in love with, what you would be passionate about, and even the personality you have. It's your job to embrace the lessons and evolve. Instead of allowing them to get you stuck in life. The way most of us interpret our experiences makes us feel punished and victimized. I had to learn I was getting back what I was putting out in the Universe. But because I didn't understand this when I prayed, I often thought my prayers went unanswered. Turns out the whole time I was just misinterpreting the answers I was receiving.

When I prayed for strength, God gave me struggles to strengthen me. When I asked for wisdom, God placed obstacles in my path to develop my critical thinking. I begged for love and received opportunities to care for those in need. And when I asked God to get me out of a terrible situation, I was left alone. This was to show me that I could save myself. Once I allowed myself to accept that life isn't happening to me, it's happening for me and embraced my life experiences as my guru, the answers to my prayers both past and present appeared.

It wasn't easy for me to accept this new way of thinking because I didn't think I was worthy of it. The idea that my life experiences had been designed to nurture my personal and spiritual development seemed too incredible. I had grown so accustomed to fighting and surviving through my experiences that I started to look forward to the punishment. I accepted that my burden was always going to be heavier and convinced myself my shoulders were wide enough to carry it. The only issue was feeling stuck, unfulfilled, and not progressing. As I shifted my thinking and my beliefs about how this whole life experience works, the first ah-ha moments came to me about many of my past experiences.

I looked back at all my failures and realized I had gotten up every time I was knocked down. Every obstacle overcome made me wiser and more prepared for the next. All the times I thought I had failed were just falls and I could always get back up. Now, looking back at the falls, they were bread crumbs telling me I was on the right path. There were times when I suffered many falls at once. It should've been a sign that a win was coming. Learning that what we perceive as failures are just necessary lessons on the way to success pushed me to dream bigger and fall more. I mean falling from the sense of taking a leap. There's an entire era of my life where it seems all I did was take huge leaps of faith back-to-back. With each leap, I believed more and more that I could fly.

So many of us go to our graves with so much left in us. When we deny ourselves the opportunity to take a leap, we leave our hopes and dreams stranded in our hearts to rot away. This is why so many die on their deathbeds with a broken heart and full of regret. We'd rather live with regret than take a leap because we don't believe in ourselves.

You are enough to be your own hero. But you have to be brave enough to discover what superpowers lie within you. Some of us are afraid of our own greatness. Marianne Williamson said, "Our deepest fear is not that we are inadequate. Our deepest fear is that we are powerful beyond measure. We ask ourselves who I am to be brilliant, gorgeous, talented, fabulous? Actually, who are you not to be? You are a child of God. Your playing small does not serve the world. There is nothing enlightened about shrinking so that other people won't feel insecure around you."

How many times have you held back or shrunk yourself because you didn't want someone to feel small? Or held back sharing your dreams or good news because you knew it would bring out other's insecurities? This often plays out with the person projecting their fears on you. We deny ourselves our own greatness so others won't feel insecure about not going after theirs. Life is hard enough dealing with our own insecurities. Don't burden yourself by trying to shoulder everyone else's. Be your own biggest fan and fall in love with your authentic self.

My greatest accomplishment in life is I know exactly who and what I am and I accept every part of me with the intention of evolving it all. I accept my flaws, my weird shit, my introverted nature, the pace at which I learn, and who I was compared to who I am today.

Take ownership of who you are. Don't allow anyone or anything to dictate how you carry out the vision you have for your life. This is your human experience. Own it. The best way we can do that is by cracking open our life experiences and pulling out the wisdom like a fortune cookie.

Thank you for going on this journey with me. Even the process of writing this book has unveiled additional wisdom and ah-ha moments I wasn't aware of before. I hope my insights and stories have inspired you to turn inward and begin your own journey of self-discovery. The process of self-discovery is not always comfortable because we often come into contact with parts of ourselves we don't want to lay claim to. OWN IT ALL. You deserve to live life more abundantly, but the only way you can do that is by being your true self.

I'd like to give you a few takeaways to help you along your journey:

The best first step is to change your thinking around the things that aren't getting you the results you desire. Thoughts become physical things. Every great idea from electricity to the internet began in the imagination. That concept is no different when we look at our life experiences. It's not just about what happens to us. It's also about how we perceive and respond that dictates how we feel about each experience.

Just because you change your thoughts doesn't mean the weight of your traumas will instantly go away. Changing our thinking requires vigilance because thoughts create beliefs that are like computer programming. It takes time to overwrite an old program and replace it with a new upgraded version. You won't instantly lose 100 pounds or get rich or happy. But once you get in alignment with your desires, you will begin to see those things manifest in your life.

My second takeaway. You must get into alignment with your desires. Thoughts alone are not enough to transform our lives. Our thoughts, words, feelings, and actions must be in total alignment. Otherwise, they will ultimately cancel each other out. If you think positive, speak negativity and feel sad, this misalignment prevents any happiness from forming in your life. So constantly check your alignments. Make sure they're supporting each other. This takes time and effort. Eventually, all the old patterns and beliefs will be replaced with those aligned with your desires.

My last takeaway is to get off the stage and become a conscious observer of your life experiences. On the stage, we're actors playing a role and can't break character. We fall into alignment with identities that don't support our growth and responses that keep us stuck. We're constantly reacting with programmed responses because we have a script to follow. Every day the same play. No room for improvisation or change in the storyline creates boredom and frustration. This is what many of us go through with our life experiences: breakups, work-life, dealing with grief, disappointments, opportunities, and love.

Next time, snatch yourself off the stage and become an audience member. It widens your perspective about your own life. It removes the bias and raises awareness. You'll notice that instead of being reactive and mechanical, you'll be more receptive and observational about what is happening. And clarity will suddenly clear away all the brain fog, allowing you to see the wisdom that was always there. This doesn't change what happened. It changes how you perceive and respond to what happens going forward and that is life changing.

Q & A

Why this book?

I realized the lessons I've learned can serve others. The framework I used to understand my life experiences gives anyone struggling to figure out where to start their healing journey, guidance to begin.

Why now?

During the pandemic, many of us were forced to sit with our thoughts when the world shutdown for almost three years. For some, this was terrifying. The idea of having to face the ramblings in our minds because we can't keep ourselves busy forced us to confront issues we've been avoiding like unworthiness, a husband we don't love anymore, childhood trauma, etc. Now that the wounds have been revealed, it's time to heal.

What keeps you going in your darkest moments?

I understand that darkness forces us to discover our own light. It may be uncomfortable, but it pushes us to evolve parts of ourselves that are undeveloped. So, the idea of growing and becoming more whole pushes me to move forward despite the darkness.

How can I apply this to my own life?

Take a moment and sit down to write out all the pivotal moments of your life, including traumas and triumphs. Next, evaluate parts of your personality that you want to develop. Then, cross-examine your personality with your traumas and triumphs to see how they have affected each other. What lessons did you miss from your life experiences?

Is it possible to get conscious enough to apply this during an experience?

Most definitely. But it requires diligent practice with every thought, experience, feeling, and action. Be patient with the process. It's not Amazon Prime. It won't be delivered in two days. But if you're fully committed to your expansion, it will come. It always does.

Is there always wisdom in every life situation?

Always. It's not always fortune cookie wisdom, but there is always a lesson with every experience to grow and expand you.

Everything from senseless violence to deceit in relationships reveals some form of wisdom.

What do I do now?

Invest in the greatest investment there is, YOU. You can do this by committing yourself to put in the work on a minute-by-minute basis. This leads to self-discovery, self-mastery, and a higher version of yourself. Also grab the journal I made for this book and visit *www.lifeismyguru.com* to get a free download to start your journey and take my questionnaire.

KEEP IN TOUCH!

@doctorholistic

@drbobbyjprice

@drbobbyprice

@drbobbyprice

Printed in the USA
CPSIA information can be obtained
at www.ICGtesting.com
JSHW022123180224
57506JS00002B/3

9 780999 612422